Notice From the Publisher

☐ If you did not receive this book as a part of a complete set of tapes and software, you only have half the tools you need to succeed. Write for a catalogue and we will also send you a *FREE RECORDABLE LEGAL FORM* to use with your first option. Write the author, Bernard Hale Zick, CCIM at Post Office Box 6399, Kingwood, Texas 77325-6399

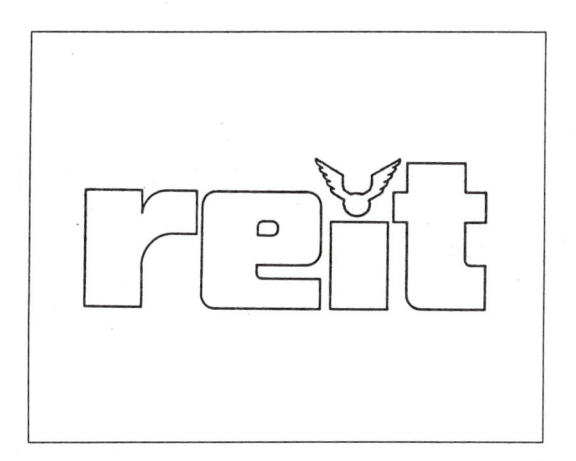

REIT Corporation

P.O. Box 6399

Kingwood, Tx 77325-6399

(800) 999-0488

Publisher

ISBN 1-886817-00-6

Hidden Profits Through Real Estate Options

How to Acquire Immediate Cash Profits, Cash Flow and Control Your Future Wealth

by Bernard Zick, CCIM

THIS BOOK IS INTENDED TO GIVE THE BEST POSSIBLE ADVICE RELATING TO REAL ESTATE OPTIONS. HOWEVER, THE AUTHOR IS NOT A C.P.A. OR AN ATTORNEY AND ANYONE WISHING TO USE THE INFORMATION CONTAINED HEREIN SHOULD SEEK THEIR OWN ACCOUNTING AND LEGAL ADVICE. FURTHERMORE, ALL STATES HAVE DIFFERENT LAWS AND CASES RELATING TO OPTIONS, CONTRACTS AND REAL ESTATE IN GENERAL. A GOOD REAL ESTATE ATTORNEY FROM YOUR STATE CAN BE AN INVALUABLE AID IN ADAPTING THESE DOCUMENTS AND CONCEPTS INTO PRACTICE. THE DOCUMENTS AND FORMS CONTAINED HEREIN, ALTHOUGH TAKEN FROM ACTUAL TRANSACTIONS, SHOULD BE REVIEWED BY YOUR LOCAL ATTORNEY BEFORE YOU USE THEM.

COPYRIGHT FOR THE TAPES AND BOOK MAY, 1989 REVISED JANUARY 1995 BY: BERNARD HALE ZICK, BOX 6399, KINGWOOD, TEXAS 77325-6399.

A SPECIAL "THANK YOU" IS DUE TO ANN HANSLIP FOR HER DOZENS OF EDITS OF THIS TEXT AND DR DAVID AUSTIN WITH THE REVISION.

FOR INFORMATION ON ADDITIONAL PUBLICATIONS, OR TO RECEIVE INFORMATION ABOUT SEMINARS OR TO BOOK MR. ZICK TO SPEAK AT YOUR EDUCATIONAL EVENT, CALL (800) 999 - 0488.

FOR INFORMATION ABOUT INVESTMENT OPPORTUNITIES, CONTACT MR. ZICK AT HIS HOUSTON OR KINGWOOD, TEXAS OFFICE.

Table of Contents

Hidden Profits *Introduction*

    How to Acquire Immediate Cash Profits, Cash Flow and Control
        Your Future Wealth Through Options................................ 1
    Eleven Ways To Reap Hidden Profits With Options 2
    Wanted: A Dose Of Inflation 6

PART ONE – *Understanding Options*

What Is An Option *Chapter One*

    Definition of Option.. 13
    Advantages to Option Seller 15
    An Option Is Subordinate To All Other Rights 16
    How To Protect Your Option Position 17
    Request For Notice Of Sale 18
    Doing the Paperwork Right 20
    Legally Correct 20
    Real Estate Contract Can Become an Option 21

Sample Lease With Option *Chapter Two*

    Option Agreement... 26
    Lease Agreement 28

How To Write Option Contracts *Chapter Three*

    What Option Form Should I Use?.................................... 33
    Filling Out The Forms 33
    Does The Option Money Apply?..................................... 38
    Prohibition Against Future Borrowing............................... 39
    A Preliminary Option Agreement 39
    What Is A Notice Of Option?.. 39
    Notice Of Option - Blank... 40
    Notice Of Option - Complete..................................... 41
    Securing Your Option 42
    Length Of Option.. 43
    Notice Of Intent To Exercise 44

    Revoking Notice Of Intent... 45
    Informal Options... 46

Paying For Options   *Chapter Four*

    How Much Do You Pay For An Option?............................. 49
    How Is It Paid?... 50
    You Can Use Anything To Pay For An Option 51
    Four Ways To Set The Price... 52
    The Best Way... 55

PART TWO – *Fast Cash Techniques*

Fix—Up And Sell   *Chapter Five*

    Avoiding A Mistake.. 59
    No Double Down Payments 60
    An Option Might Be The Better Way 61
    How To Protect Yourself 61
    Solution: Have A Right To Extend.................................. 62
    Solution: Always Have Something Recordable.................... 63

Options Are Like Listings Marketing Bargains   *Chapter Six*

    Out-Of-State Listings And Clients................................... 65
    Options When Listings Are Unobtainable 68
    Brokerage Without A Real Estate License 68

Special Option Structure   *Chapter Seven*

    Getting Paid Not To Buy: An Option To Cancel The Deal 71
    Read This Section Twice. It's A Real Money Maker! The Rolling
        Option... 72
    First Right Of Refusal And Options.................................. 73

Option Solutions To Foreclosures   *Chapter Eight*

    Options & Federal Tax Liens.. 75
    Redemptive Rights Are Like Options 76
    Discounted Sale - Option To Buy Back............................. 76
    Option To Buy Back To Revalue Asset 78

How To Get Income Tax Breaks With Options   *Chapter Nine*

    An Option Is Not Taxed Until Exercised............................ 79

Profit By Selling Options - Don't Exercise Them 81
Option To Option 82
Establishing A Basis In Your Option 83

Tax And Financial Planning *Chapter Ten*

Options And Estate Freezing 85
Options And The Financial World 87
Options And Bankruptcy 88

PART THREE – *Cash Flow Techniques*

Lease Options *Chapter Eleven*

What Are Lease Options 93
Housing Prices 94
Pro Tenant Or Owner—Who Wins? 96
Lease Option/sandwich Lease 97
The Ultimate Example 98
Tips For Finding Lease Options. 99
Pro Tenant Lease With Option To Buy 99
OPTION AGREEMENT - Blank. 100
LEASE AGREEMENT - Blank. 103
OPTION AGREEMENT 107
LEASE AGREEMENT 110
Lease Options For Positive Cash Flow 114
Lease Option Pitfalls 115

Selling Lease Options *Chapter Twelve*

PART FOUR – *Long Term Profits*

Zero Interest Financing *Chapter Thirteen*

An Option Is Better Than A Loan 123
Options: A Better Way To Finance Properties 125
Options To Avoid Loan Qualifications 129
Options Are Zero Interest Loans 130
Lease With Option To Buy Zero Interest Loan 130
Options As A Financial Aid To Sellers. 125

Control And Other Uses   *Chapter Fourteen*

    Motive: No Profit, Just Control 135
    Avoiding Ordinary Tax On Quick Sale Of Options 135
    Options & Due-on-sale 136
    Options As A Geographical Asset 139

Equity Sharing Option   *Chapter Fifteen*

    The Players / Their Roles. 141
    Tenant With Option / Equity Participation. 142
    More Lease / Option Opportunities 144
    No Negative Cash Flow With Lease / Option 145
    Equity Participation Limitations 145
    Buying Half A House. 145
    Advertisements That Work 148
    Mom Buys Half Son Buys Half 148
    Four More Combinations 149
    Think About This One 150
    You Live Rent Free 150
    H.E.L.P. 151
    Owner Benefits 153

Estate Building With Down Payment Partners   *Chapter Sixteen*

    Matching Needs. 159
    Working With Others. 160

Two DBA Agreements   *Chapter Seventeen*

    An Informal Agreement. 185
    The Lawyers' Version 188

Syndicating Options   *Chapter Eighteen*

    Joint Venture Options. 197
    Partnership Agreement 198

Shared Appreciation Mortgages   *Chapter Nineteen*

    You Can Do It With An Option 203

                                                                                                                                                       Chapter Twenty

                                                                                                                                                                             POSTSCRIPT

Introduction

Hidden Profits

How to Acquire Immediate Cash Profits, Cash Flow and Control Your Future Wealth Through Options

There is a romance to the concept of dealing with options. Visions of high finance and sophisticated investors come to mind! Most people see the topic as mysterious, when in fact, most people have more knowledge about the subject than they realize, from everyday common sense.

Options can control vast wealth and serve as a strategic investment tool. Options need not be "mysterious" or reserved just for the affluent—because the fact is, **options are a perfect tool for all levels of investing.**

The option is an under—utilized and most powerful investing tool. It can provide the option holder with many of the benefits of ownership without the headaches. Options allow for control, control of future, potential profits and potential ownership. And a most important factor, various option programs can generate cash flow, money to live on. For those interested in building wealth, control of real property through options can be arranged without the heavy negative cash flow burdens associated with most other creative acquisition methods. It is a planning tool, a strategy.

There are three dramatic uses of an option. The first is *quick turn profits*. The second is *cash flow producing programs*. Lastly, the classic use of options is for *long term wealth* that is accomplished by FIXING THE PURCHASE PRICE AT A FUTURE DATE DURING PERIODS OF APPRECIATION, (both appreciation from inflation or from demand for a particular area.) Looking at current, long term trends, the future may well hold several periods of appreciation and if so, this text is well timed.

Properly structured, **long term options still show profits with mild appreciation and often major gains just from the pay down of the loan.** Fully amortized loans include a small amount of principal in each payment in the early years of the loan. As time passes, this amount increases. If you have a long term lease option on a property with, say, 15 years left on a 30 year loan, the paydown would be significant.

Furthermore as the loan is paid down the gap between the existing loan balance and the property's market value increases. Forces driving up the market value include: appreciation, property upgrades, usage changes, scarcity of similar properties, rezoning and the like.

Options are no more difficult to obtain or negotiate than any other creative financing tool. And, they are more clearly defined in law than some of the newer techniques, such as selling a half interest in a house to the tenant.

This book can show you how to obtain cash profits now, continuing cash flow and long term wealth through the use of options. The programs are various. The applications are limitless, and the profit can be tremendous.

These techniques will work with or without inflation. They will work with very little cash, but can also be a powerful tool for the wealthy investor. There has never been a person with a sincere desire to profit from investing, nor a time in history, when options wouldn't have worked.

First of all, the investor must become familiar with all the techniques and applications. **Then you will start noticing opportunities.** To that end, this text is designed.

Eleven Ways To Reap Hidden Profits With Options

Three Categories

As stated earlier, options are the most powerful and dynamic investing tool available today. Once you have mastered option knowledge, you will find applications for it in every facet of business, industry and finance. The stock market and real estate fields implement option techniques extensively. There are profits to be made in stock market options, **but I am more excited about what can be done with real estate options**.

Stock market options are cash intensive and short term in nature. *Real estate options can be structured for small investors to use for short term or long term profits, as well as cash flow.* And, in many instances it is not necessary to have a great deal of cash to reap these benefits.

Based on the type of profit options generate, I have broken option strategy into three categories. The first category is **"Fast Cash Techniques."** These are techniques where the option is used to control a property long enough for you to pass it on to another person at a profit.

The second category, **"Cash Flow Techniques,"** uses the option to generate monthly income for twelve months or for years into the future. They're dynamic concepts that can give you a cash flow to live on, buying you the freedom to quit your job and have more control over your own life.

The third category is **"Long Term Wealth Building Option Techniques."** These techniques, blended with the long term advantages of real estate, will allow you to build a healthy net worth without many of the hassles associated with day—to—day ownership of real estate.

Arranging hidden profits. On the surface it appears that the owner of real estate has all the benefits of the property. However, there could be dozens of profit opportunities that have been given away to an option holder, hidden from the casual observer's view. Maintaining a low profile while controlling wealth—generating assets appeals to many people today, especially those intent on personal privacy.

Also, **many property owners are shortsighted and don't see the hidden benefits.** For instance, the inflation rate as measured by the Consumer Price Index during 1985 and into 1989 was quite low. By and large, investors tend to forget about the potential of real estate appreciation during such periods. Long term appreciation is still there and the threat of high inflation rates has not totally gone away. **This sort of profit is hidden because it is ignored.** It is hidden because investors use short term criteria even when they are involved in long term investments like real estate.

Options can reveal hidden profits for you when integrated into the solution of another person's real estate problems. Example: if the owner of a property DOES need depreciation but CAN'T HANDLE management, ownership of his property could be a major headache, with or without positive cash flow. **The hidden profits are in property management and leasing of the units** that the current owner can't handle. With a well—conceived program, such as the use of lease options, these hidden profits could be yours.

Let's review the three categories of profit potential one more time, to point out the ELEVEN WAYS YOU CAN GAIN FROM THE USE OF OPTIONS. By highlighting the list at the beginning of the text, you will be alerted to how each idea fits into the total picture.

A. Fast Cash Techniques

There are 3 fast cash techniques. The first is as old as the oldest investor, that is, **(1) "Fix Up And Sell."** This is the process of finding properties in need of repair that can be acquired at a price that has been discounted far more than the cost of doing the repairs.

There are three steps to the process of being a renovation specialist.

1. The first step is to learn to acquire properties under advantageous pricing terms (advantageous to you). These terms must allow you the freedom to do the things you need to do to make a profit. The option is an excellent way to control the properties you are working on.

2. The second step is the renovation process itself.

3. The third is the marketing of the properties. The process of renovation is beyond the scope of this text but we will talk about the technical aspects of selling properties you have under option.

We call the second fast cash technique **(2) "Options Are Like Listings—Marketing Bargains."** Real estate agents involved in larger commercial transactions receive relatively healthy fees for their services. But being an agent comes with a certain amount of liabilities and the increase in court cases against real estate agents makes an investor think twice before getting a license. YOU can reap the same benefits that an agent does. In fact sometimes you can make unusually large profits in the marketing of properties that wouldn't be given to a real estate agent, **by learning how to control properties that sellers want to sell through real estate options.**

The third fast cash technique is **(3) "Use Options To Profit in Foreclosures."** Foreclosures are the most interesting bargains! You can get paid for **not** buying foreclosures. We will show you how to tie a property up in such a way that you either obtain the property at a substantial discount—a price far below what most people would consider a bargain purchase—or you get paid for not buying it. I can't imagine anything more exciting than getting paid for not buying property.

Options work perfectly when you are working with foreclosures. Going into title on properties in the middle of foreclosure is a rather hazardous experience unless you are a real expert. There are all kinds of real and implied liabilities. However, beginning and professional investors quite often approach the foreclosure market through real estate options. This is a great method to use to tie up future profits and to nail down performance expectations, (the second party performs as he is supposed to), so you are able to make your profit. This can work with lenders or owners who are "under the gun." And the option can be structured in such a way that everybody benefits.

B. Options For Cash Flow

Fourth on our list would be **(4) "Straight Lease Options."** Most everyone has heard of a "Lease With Option to Buy" or "Lease Purchase." Home buyers and sellers talk about it and it's often used in newspaper ads selling properties. *But, very few people fully understand the power of lease options to control not only future price but current cash flow.*

Lease options can change the long term ownership of real estate from a system where you lose money month by month in the early ownership into a more desirable situation with a break—even or positive cash flow from day one on!

In addition to the straight lease option, which is technique #4, there is a sophisticated technique known as the **(5)—"Sandwich Lease Option"**. With a Sandwich Lease Option you not only get the benefits of cash flow, you get long term benefits! Once the initial work is done, there is little to do but sit back and collect the checks.

A sandwich lease option broadens the number of people you can deal with. In the case of a normal lease option you deal with a tenant who might want to become a buyer. With the sandwich lease option, you may deal with tenants who are interested in becoming buyers or buyers who are looking for a creative way of acquiring property.

Thus, technique #4 is a lease option with you as the owner and someone else as the tenant. With technique #5, the sandwich lease option, you control the property through a lease option and either lease it to another or lease option it to another or better yet, sell it to another person.

The sixth technique has to do with **(6) "Selling Leased Property."** That's right! If you think you can make money selling what you own, just wait until you learn to sell what you don't own! This technique gives you both cash flow and fast cash.

C. Long Term Hidden Profits

The seventh technique is what I call **(7) "The Pure Option."** If you have the right to buy a property at a fixed price, you can obtain any future appreciation. Pure options have made fortunes for people and they can do the same for you.

Options can be used to control property for **(8) "Rezoning and Development."** One of the quickest ways to make "large dollars" in real estate investing is to change the use of the property. Developers will tell you that if you can increase the utility of a property, like converting a house that you rent to a tenant to a house zoned for a small shop, you greatly increase the rental income. When you rent to a merchant you can charge a higher rate.

The lease option can be used as part of the long—term wealth building process as well as for cash flow as stated earlier. It can be a desirable tool to control future profits even if the cash flow isn't generated on a month—to—month basis with the lease option. As a ninth technique, options can provide the same function as **(9) "Zero Interest Financing."** If you think there is profit in buying real estate when you pay interest —wait until you learn how to buy it without paying any interest at all!

Next is an exotic concept known as the **(10) "Equity Share Lease Option."** As a property owner you'd rather give a prospective tenant/buyer a straight lease option. This way the tenant has some benefits of future appreciation. But the standard lease option doesn't work in a lot of circumstances. This is especially true in higher priced properties.

You used to be able to say to the tenant, "Pay me an extra $50 per month and I'll add an option to buy with your lease." Nowadays it takes an additional

$300 to $400 to make a property break even and it's hard to convince most people to sign the standard lease option. The "Equity Share Lease Option" helps solve the problems caused by today's prices.

We call it our **H.E.L.P.** agreement. **H.E.L.P.** stands for **H**omeowner **E**quity **L**ease **P**articipation and we believe you'll find it to be a very sophisticated and exciting concept.

Concept eleven deals with the use of **(11) "Options in Syndicating Real Estate and the Syndication of Options."** There is a lot of money to be made in the syndication of real estate. There is also profit from holding shares in syndications. The option is an integral part of putting together these long—term transactions.

Wouldn't you be foolish to agree to buy something that you couldn't afford? Doesn't it make more sense to have an option to buy that property until you get the money put together? Options and syndications provide hidden profits in deals you thought were unobtainable.

Whether you are interested in a short—term or long—term option to purchase a piece of property, sometimes the option costs a lot more money than you have available. Why not try syndicating the option? Get a group of investors together to put up the money to buy the option. Long—term profits that seemed hidden to you before are now available.

Wanted: A Dose Of Inflation

Do you need massive inflation to make real estate options profitable? Obviously not, when you use options to control properties for short—term profits. You also can get maximum cash flow and control of properties with various cash flow formulas such as the "Lease Option," the "Sandwich Lease Option," and selling lease option properties on contract for deed.

But what about long—term appreciation? At this point it is important to discuss inflation and how it affects real estate today.

To begin with, it is hard to determine the **real** inflation rate. What index do you use? Cities in the same state experience vastly different appreciation rates—inflation or not.

If you measure inflation by the Consumer Price Index, it is down to approximately 3-4%. This has been a level the Federal Reserve has striven to reach for years. They say our economy moves along quite well at the 3 to 6% level. THREE TO SIX PERCENT IS NOT ZERO INFLATION, however!

So, if you buy a $100,000 piece of property that appreciates at 3%/year, it would be worth $116,000 in 5 years or $134,000 in 10 years. That may not seem like much, but let's make some assumptions.

A knowledgeable real estate investor, who is willing to put in the amount of time needed to find a good buy, will buy at 10% below true market value. So he would buy the property for $90,000. In addition, *a Barney Zick student will buy the property for very little money down*—say $10,000. Now just because you can show a profit of $45,000 after 10 years with a 10% investment may not be reason enough to run out and buy the property today. NO, the current 3% inflation factor is not reason enough to buy properties—but it is a positive factor combined with the ability to purchase real barg**ains**, through diligent searching for the right property and the ability to finance with no negative cash flow (because of current low interest rates —compared to the early 1980's—and YOUR CREATIVE FINANCING SKILLS — such as the use of lease options).

Secondly, is the inflation rate in real estate actually 3%? Remember the statistician who drowned crossing the river with an average depth of 3 inches? I'm sure there are readers in Long Island who would like to find the person who bought their lovely 3—bedroom house 5 years ago—and have increased the price equal to the Consumer Price Index. Just because the nation's consumer goods as measured by the price index are moving along at 3% doesn't mean that the real estate in your home town is moving along at 3%.

In some areas in the country, prices for real estate have been escalating an average of 15 to 20% over the last several years. In some cities, prices have been going down during the same time frame. Averages are made to help you spot overall trends, not make decisions on specific properties and locales.

Thirdly, are we trying to guess the speed of the car by measuring the width of the tires? Does the Consumer Price Index (or any index) measure what is happening with real estate prices? The CPI is probably a poor measure of anything except for the cost of living, if you are a renter.

You see, President Reagan needed to slow down the CPI in his first administration. He was elected on the promise of reducing inflation. He asked the boys with the green eye shades in the census bureau what was pushing prices up. They told him that one factor was increasing housing prices. So he told them to take the price of the average house off the Consumer Price Index. When they asked what to put in that blank space, he said he didn't care — just use anything you want that doesn't move up as fast as housing.

Although the above conversation is hypothetical, the results were not. The census bureau decided to use the cost of the average RENTAL UNIT in the CPI instead of the average home. They were justified in doing so. The census bureau explained that in the future the average person couldn't afford to purchase the average house! This would be a change from historic patterns because the U.S. has been the one country on this earth in which the majority of its people owned their own homes. We are going to slip to lower than the 50% mark in the 1990s. That was their justification for using rental units instead.

The fact is rents have NEVER(at least I've not seen it in 20 years) gone up as fast as housing prices. In any nation in the world you'll find housing prices so high that only the elite can afford to own the property they live in. Everyone else rents at a rate that fits into the average for that country.

So, although the consumer price index is the popular one used by the press, it is an extremely poor one to measure how real estate is doing. There are others. The FHA reports the average price of the average sale of an FHA house, but that doesn't tell you what the upper bracket homes are doing. However, many homes are too expensive to qualify for FHA financing.

You could look at the average price of a newly constructed home— that's been going up every year. Whether it's reflected in the CPI or not, increases have been in the neighborhood of 6 to 8% a year. (If you buy my argument that a 3% increase in property is helpful to a real estate investor, the true average increase in U.S. housing of 6% or higher has to be even better!)

As I pointed out, appreciation rates vary from area to area, from neighborhood to neighborhood and from property type to property type. Perhaps you need to do a little investigating to see what is actually going up and what isn't. *What if you live in an area with zero inflation?* Well, if properties are going down, I wouldn't be a hot and heavy investor. **I might lease option properties for the long term and lease them out again to get higher positive cash flow.** The option would be an insurance policy in case inflation catches hold. Or I might be a buyer and seller of notes and deeds of trust. But, if properties were actually going down, I'D MOVE!!

Now, if they go down for one month, that's not the time to call the U—Haul—It folks. But if they go down for a period of time and you don't expect any change for 3 to 5 years down the line, and you have nothing else keeping you there, there are lots of roads out of town. (In most communities this won't be the case. In most, there is some kind of appreciation or inflation.)

Next. **Do we need inflation at all?** Some areas will increase in value because of overall inflation and some because more and more people want to live there. In the late 1980's San Diego honestly suffered from growth. Too many people wanted to live here compared to what's available. And it has kept prices up in some parts of town and pushed them up in others. But let's assume the worst case scenario for the entire country. Prices aren't going to go up at least for awhile— and perhaps never.

So, Is Real Estate A Good Investment? I believe so. Here's why.

1. **Your tenant pays off your loan.** If you buy real estate and rent it out, over a period of time the rents received will deliver the property unto you free and clear.

2. **Real estate is a tax shelter.** Yes, they have cut down the number of tax shelters each investor gets, but real estate is still a tax shelter. That means that the money this particular investment makes won't be taxed to you at this time.

3. **You can still borrow against it.** Maybe gold won't be a good investment. Nobody's loaning you 75 cents on the dollar for gold. If you could borrow it, you'd have to search out such a lender. Every other corner in town has an institution that makes real estate loans.

4. On the assumption that you do want to invest for your future, (call it savings if you will), **isn't it smart to put your savings into something that's a good inflation hedge, should inflation return? Real estate is one of the best.**

5. **You can manage it yourself and control its destiny.** Or, if you like to buy into bigger deals, you can hire professional management. Either case has its advantages.

6. **Because every property is unique, the more knowledge you have, the better you are at buying it.** If you become extremely knowledgeable and are willing to spend the appropriate amount of time to search out bargains, you can build a large net worth each time you buy right. The list goes on. There's a strong case for real estate at zero inflation rate.

I have one tremendous advantage as your real estate advisor. I have been at this for nearly 20 years. Beginning investors have yet to see or perhaps have gone through one cycle of bad times and only have one set of solutions for problems. Maybe that's the reason you become so conservative the longer you invest. The trick is to be conservative and remain optimistic as I am. Some people may say I'm crazy to say that inflation may return. I don't know whether I'm optimistic or just realistic. When interest rates were low, we never dreamed they'd go to 18 to 22%. When we were at that plateau we said they'd never get as low as they are now. Nothing is absolute. Things change or cycle constantly.

There's an old man named Templeton who runs some mutual funds. I think his investment is good enough that I've put cash into his mutual funds. In a recent interview with reporters he predicted that in the not so distant future we'd be back to double digit inflation. **In my heart of hearts I believe that.** No predictions. I'm just saying that someday we'll be back to heavy inflation. Those folks who have taken the current low interest rate to refinance their current holdings or unloaded their "going nowhere" holdings—and repositioned themselves for a long—term loan at low inflation rates, will be really excited if inflation rates come back.

If you are one of those people who think it's time to get off of the train just because it ran out of fuel, don't come complaining to me several years down the line when you wake up to realize that the train crept out of the station.

What's in this book will work with or without inflation. But with inflation, options are the tool of future riches.

Part One

Understanding Options

Chapter One

What Is An Option

Definition of Option

Contractually, an option is the right to acquire the bundle of rights known as real estate. It is a contractual agreement.

The property owner is called "the optionor." The buyer of the option is called "the optionee."

With an option, THE OPTIONEE HAS THE **RIGHT TO BUY, OR LEASE,** BUT **NOT THE OBLIGATION.** The optionor is **obligated** to sell under the terms of the option. That's right, obligated. Once he (or she) has given you an option, he *has* to sell to you as per the option terms. This one sided arrangement differs from a sale's contract or real estate purchase agreement.

The option is a unilateral agreement, (one way). The real estate purchase contract is a bilateral, (two way), agreement. You might consider the option a seller's irrevocable offer to sell. The option holder can make the property owner sell. The property owner (optionor) can't make the optionee buy. Once "exercised," once the buyer says "Yes, I want to buy," a bilateral contract is formed which either party can enforce.

EXAMPLE: On July 1st you read a newspaper ad for a gold watch. It is perfect. And although it is an expensive watch, priced at $1,295, it is a bargain compared to prices for the same watch elsewhere.

You go down to the store at 4:00 p.m. on the last day of the three—day Fourth of July sale. You have cash for the purchase, but they are sold out and instead you receive a rain check, good for six months.

On July 18th, your birthday, your receive your dream watch as a gift. A relative had seen the same ad and decided to be generous. Since you assume you will never need the rain check, you just toss it in your top desk drawer.

At Christmas time your boss notices your watch and says that he wants to get the same one for his son. He asks you to check on the current price for him. You call all over town and learn that the going price then is $1,895. There are no sales.

At this point you remember your rain check! That rain check is an OPTION to buy that style of watch at $1,295. The rain check holder has the "not—to—be—denied" right to buy until December. Doesn't that really make the value of the OPTION/rain check $600?

Now you have several choices. You can give the rain check to your boss and collect "atta boy points" or you could sell it to him for $100, 200, $300, up to $599. Or you could not reveal the fact that you hold the rain check, ask him to give you $1,895 and you could go buy the watch for $1,295. Or, you could give him the rain check and *hope* he offers to split the profit. In any case, the OPTION gives you control and profit (cash flow) potential.

Webster defines an option as: 4. the right, acquired for a consideration, to buy, sell or lease something at a fixed price, sign or renew a contract etc. within a specified time.

The Arnold Encyclopedia of Real Estate defines an OPTION as: the right for which a consideration has been paid to buy, lease or sell a particular piece of real estate to or from another at a specified price and within a designated period.

An OPTIONEE is one who holds an option, i.e., a right, for which he has paid a consideration, to buy specified property from another within a specified period of time and at a specified price or to sell such property to such other person at a specified price and within a specified time.

Options are not restricted to purchases and sales. For example, an optionee may want to lease property, rather than purchase property.

An OPTIONER or OPTIONOR, is one who grants an option to another. In real estate, the optionor usually grants, for a valuable consideration, the exclusive right to purchase a specific property, at a specified price and during a specified period of time.

Let me weave a little story to explain the legal definition.

In a law library you could take one of three aisles. Aisle one is Old English Law, aisle two is UCC (Uniform Commercial Code) and aisle number three is Contract Law. Problems sometimes arise when you have a situation found on both or all three aisles. One set of law will say one thing and the other set of law will say another, concerning individual rights and the law. This is contractual law. It is a contract which gives you the right to buy the bundle of rights known as real estate and the laws concerning real estate are covered by Old English Law.

Chapter One

What Is An Option

A friend of mine, a real estate attorney, says "A legally valid option is written either independently or as a part of a lease, with specific requirements which must be contained in the option.

"Since the option itself is a contract, it must meet all the basic requirements of any contract and be legally enforceable independent of any collateral document. This means there must be: **(1)** a definite description of the property that is the subject of the option; **(2)** specific terms regarding price, duration of option and payment of purchase price; **(3)** consideration in the form of money, services or other obligations. Be sure to make the terms specific and enumerate what the consideration is. Avoid vague first refusal" clauses.

"Additional specifications may be built into the option, such as prohibition of transfer of the option or an increasing purchase price as the term of the option approaches expiration. Such a provision would encourage an optionee to purchase before the price went up any higher.

"Options may also be conditioned upon performance of other agreements such as leases. So a breach of the lease could terminate the option — another incentive for leasees to pay their rent on time."

This discussion is directed to option buyers. Before we go much further, let's briefly review the advantages to the seller, which will be more fully discussed when appropriate within the text.

Advantages to Option Seller

1. **Tax free.** Probably the number one reason a seller will sell an option to buy is because the money he gets is his to spend and tax free <u>at the time of receipt.</u> It's taxability is deferred until the option is exercised, expires, or vacated.

2. If he received money as a down payment, a seller would have to pay capital gains taxes. Thus, **options can delay paying taxes**.

3. With a sale, there is quite often a commission to be paid. Most options are negotiated directly and thus the **seller saves the price of a commission.**

4. As a tax timing tool, **a seller can pick the year in which he or she wants to be taxed!** This will be especially important to high tax bracket sellers.

5. If the seller needs money, a tax free approach would be to borrow it. But, there would be loan costs, points and the like. And **a loan has to be repaid! (But not an option.)**

6. If the **optionor** was living in or using the property on which the option is placed, he **wouldn't have to move** out. Odds are that he would have to move if a sale was made.

Chapter One

7. If the optionor is facing foreclosure, this could be the only way to receive money to stop the foreclosure and not have an added debt burden — plus he would be allowed to stay on the property.

I don't want to take a lot of time here to make a full and comprehensive list of "seller benefits." But, so many people assume that an option benefits the buyer only, that a partial list of seller benefits seems appropriate at this point.

As we explore options, details on the benefits to all parties will be expanded upon and other values revealed. For now, we'll simply state that options are so flexible that they help buyers, sellers and others gain *mutual* benefits.

An Option Is Subordinate To All Other Rights

"It's all mine. I own it free and clear!"

Owning real property without debts attached is a desirable goal. But no one really owns property without "strings." Since way back in old English history, a gift of land from the king was to be repaid with loyalty and annual tax payments.

Today, your property is not only "subject to" annual tax assessments, but judgments made as a result of various court cases have limited your rights to the use of your property. For instance, zoning laws limit use. Air rights have been challenged when the height of your proposed building might block out someone's ocean view or the path of an airport runway.

Further rights are relinquished with an option — for an option is "behind" or subordinate to all other rights given away to lenders.

Here's a layman's view of the complexities involved. An option is a unilateral contract. That means the power to make or require something to happen only goes one way, (vs. bilateral). I can make you give me the property as long as I perform, (pay, give notices, etc.), as we wrote it in our option contract. My option is a claim against the real estate. *But it is a claim that is subordinate to all other rights already given away on the property.*

Our option position is secondary to all other liens filed against the property before you. And if the owner doesn't pay his property taxes, that lien will be put before your interest too!

For instance, if there is a first AND second mortgage on the property, the option is subordinate to them. If the person who owns the property does not pay the first and second, you, the option holder, may have to go to the courthouse

> There are advantages to the seller in giving an option.

steps to protect your option. The person there at the courthouse steps will say, "Do I have any offers on this property?"

The second mortgage holder will say, "Well, I bid the amount of the first mortgage and the amount of the second."

The sheriff or trustee will say, "Do I hear any more offers on this property?" And you'll yell, "BUT, I HAVE AN OPTION."

The sheriff will say, "Going once." And you'll say, "I've got an option." He then says, "SOLD! to the second mortgage holder." — "But I had an option."

Your option is wiped out at foreclosure. Why? Because they have the rights that are superior before yours.

How do you protect yourself? In lots of ways.

How To Protect Your Option Position

An option is very much like a second mortgage because it is usually a secondary claim against assets. Keeping that fact in mind might help you remember what to do with an option.

What do we do to protect our position if we hold a second mortgage? Very simple.

1. You do all the title research work. Obtain a preliminary title report from a title insurance company. **This will allow you to confirm what rights have already been given away.** If you decide to buy the policy, within limits, its accuracy is guaranteed.

2. Whenever I get an option I always want to get a notice of default filed, so if there is ever a default on the first and the second I know about it in a hurry. (Not all areas of the country have this. Call your county recorder's office and ask about this.) This technique is common practice when you acquire a second mortgage. If a notice of default is on file at the county recorder's office and a default is filed on any lien currently on that property, you will receive a duplicate notice of default.

3. Next, I want to get the first and second mortgage holder to give me the right to make payments if the title holder misses one. I want to set up a system so that I am notified if the person who owns the property hasn't made the payments.

4. I like to put a "slight punishment" in my option agreement if the property owner allows the property to go into foreclosure. Punishments are not enforceable in contracts, but here's what I mean.

EXAMPLE: You have a $100,000, 7—acre ranch in the south part of town and I have an option to buy it from you for $100,000. I say to you, "I'm paying you $10,000 for the option and the option is good for five years at $100,000. There's a first mortgage on this property of about $60,000."

I may ask, "Are you going to make payments on that first mortgage." If you are the title holder of the property, you are going to say that, "Yes I am. But don't worry, I'm not going to let that mortgage go into default."

I then point out that "if you let the lien secured by this property go into default, not only will you lose your $40,000 equity, I'll lose my option and the $10,000 I paid for it."

To protect myself, I add a clause to the option that says if the owner ever does let the property go into default and foreclosure is filed, instead of paying $40,000 for the remaining equity, I pay $1,000. *We call that $1,000.00 liquidated damages. After that, I just take over the ownership.*

The owner would probably gasp and say he couldn't do that. Well, remind him, he was the guy who said he would never let the loan go into default. Maybe you'll have to negotiate more than a $1,000 settlement in your agreement. Somewhere between $1,000 and $40,000 would be a happy medium. But remember this point. If you put a clause in there that says if the property ever goes into default and

---

Capital National Mortgage
Loan Processing Dept.
1000 Lenders Way
Middleville, KS 66215

RE: Loan #152-604-752
Address: 9222 Happy Drive
Middleville, KS 66215

Dear Mr. Lender:

We have entered into an agreement with Bernard Zick, (address: P O Box 630, Solana Beach, CA 92075.), concerning the subject property. Therein, we have agreed to continue making timely payments on the note due you.

Please, henceforth, send Mr. Zick a duplicate notice of delinquent payment, should I ever be in arrears.

This will not only comply with the terms of my agreement with Mr. Zick, but will give you one more interested party to look after the loans.

Very truly yours,

Ima Borrower

foreclosure is filed that you can step in and **pick up the equity by paying the owner much less than originally agreed** — you've just put in a strong incentive to make sure that foreclosures never jeopardize your option.

5. I also like to use another protective clause. I got this idea from wrap-around mortgages. If I ever receive a notice of delinquent payment I can make that payment myself, so the property doesn't go into default — and *I get credit for $3 off the option price for every $1 I pay in his behalf.*

So, if I owe him $40,000 to exercise the option and he goes along for a year or so not making that first mortgage, pretty soon I don't owe him any more money! I get $3 credit for every $1 I have to pay, because I'm being forced to step out of my role as an option holder and start making payments.

If you ever use this idea, send a xerox of your check and a letter stating the 3—for—1 credit by certified mail to the optionor. This will make it easier to prove your point, if you argue later.

6. Lastly, to be warned early in the game, I ask for a **duplicate notice of**

Capital National Mortgage
Loan Processing Dept.
1000 Lenders Way
Middleville, KS 66215

RE: Loan#152-604-752
Address: 9222 Happy Drive
Middleville, KS 66215

Dear Mr. Lender:

We have entered into an agreement with Bernard Zick, (address: PO Box 630, Solana Beach, CA 92075), concerning the subject property. Therein, we have agreed to continue making timely payments on the note due you. Please, henceforth, send Mr. Zick a duplicate notice of delinquent payment, should I ever be in arrears.

This will not only comply with the terms of my agreement with Mr. Zick, but will give you one more interestd party to look after the loans.

Very truly yours,

Ima Borrower

Chapter One

delinquent payments. The benefit of requiring notification of delinquent payments, which is available in many states, is that a large delinquent loan payment build-up cannot occur without your knowledge. This is a notice you will receive prior to getting a notice of default or foreclosure.

EXAMPLE: A property is subject only to a first mortgage (or Deed of Trust) to Capital National. I would have the optionor write them a letter, like the one below.

You DO need a letter from the property owner. The lender can not release such information without written approval from the borrower.

Most computerized lenders will be happy to respond to your request. Small escrow companies might agree, but it would be smart to send them a supply of self addressed envelopes.

Doing the Paperwork Right

There are several facets of the option concept itself that you must understand. First, it is a contractual agreement. AN OPTION MUST BE FULL AND COMPLETE. No details are left undecided.

It's a unilateral, one way contract. How do I pay him? How much do I pay him? When do I pay him? How long do I have before I have to pay him? Write it so that it is complete all the way through. All your option agreements should be so complete that you could hand it to an intelligent third party and he would say that it was obvious how you closed this transaction.

I make sure that my options are drawn right. If you go to your local stationary store and ask for such a form they are likely to give you a large piece of white paper that says OPTION on the top, while the rest of the page is blank. Don't use that because you won't fill it out properly. **It is all blank space anyway!**

Just because an option is long doesn't mean that it is complete— it may or may not be well drawn. You can have a lawyer draw up a 35—page document and it will cost you a fortune. I've had a few of these drawn and learned the lesson the hard way, that long isn't always best. Using a lawyer is not a guarantee of good results. If you get a good lawyer, he'll do a good job on it and if you get a bad lawyer, you'll get a bad job. *Remember, not all lawyers understand real estate.* Now I use my own forms.

With options, you have a dual assignment. You have to negotiate for both the option and for the purchase of the property. The paperwork merges both these tasks into one written document.

Legally Correct

My real estate attorney, points out that "it is very important to be aware of the legal requirements of an option to be sure any option you agree to remains valid."

Probably the most common oversight in providing an option occurs in leases. How many times have you seen the phrase 'tenant has first refusal', in the miscellaneous section of a pre—printed lease form? You may have even seen

What Is An Option

that that phrase added to a custom— drafted lease! *Such terminology does nothing more than provide an invitation to litigate in court over the terms and conditions of any future purchase by the tenant because of its indefiniteness.* First right of refusal provides the buyer-optionee with a priority right to purchase property. First the owner gets and accepts an offer. Then he calls the person with first right of refusal. The holder of that right can buy under the same terms and conditions offered by the other purchaser and accepted by an owner.

Another crucial error, often considered unimportant but crucial according to an attorney, is the failure to mention a specific cost or "consideration" for the right to buy the property. Since the right to buy is a legally enforceable contract obligation, it must be accompanied by a corresponding benefit to the optionor, (one who offers the option), or detrimental to the optionee. The consideration is usually money, but it doesn't have to be. It could be property, services provided or any legally enforceable promise from one party to another.

Persons offering options need to be cautious that an expiration time or event is specified or they will be at the mercy of the optionee until the optionee agrees to release any rights they have to the property. If no termination point is mentioned, disputes could result years after the optionor thought the potential purchaser (optionee) declined to purchase.

Other common mistakes in offering options include: 1) failure to put it in writing when real estate is involved; it is unenforceable if it is not in writing; 2) failure to adequately describe the property and specifying a price which the seller/optionor assumes is a cash price and which the buyer/optionee assumes is an owner—financed price."

EXAMPLE: When I'm working on a small, simple transaction, quite often I'll just use a REAL ESTATE SALE'S CONTRACT and down at the bottom, in that wide space, I say, "The earnest money deposit, in paragraph 4 above, will be held by the Seller in his own account as OPTION money consideration for a closing any time within the next 12 months after this date. Time of closing will be set by the buyer. Should the buyer fail to close, the earnest money deposit will be forfeited as full and complete liquidated damages, in that exact damages are difficult if not impossible to ascertain." Never try to deceive the seller into thinking this modified contract is a normal sale. It will backfire on you if it goes to court. To be proper, be clear and have the seller initial next to words "option".

Real Estate Contract Can Become an Option

Is a real estate contract a form of an option?

No, unless you have one that's especially drawn by yourself, like we have. Most real estate contracts are bilateral agreements. You promise to sell and I promise to buy.

Chapter One

It's a firm deal as long as all contingencies have been removed.

If I don't buy, you can sue me for specific performance and possibly for compensatory damages in some circumstances. Specific performance suits brought by sellers aren't often as successful as specific performance suits brought by buyers because real estate is "unique." Supposedly, the theory is "you can find lots of buyers but I can only find one property like that property."

There are lots of "conditional" clauses. You can put these "screened door" or "subject to" clauses in your contract, such as "Subject to my partner's approval." If you put one subject—to in there, which could let you out, then you don't have a binding agreement. Once all contingencies are removed and all that is left is—"I will buy and you will sell and closing will be at such and such date," if either party does not show up at closing — the other party can sue to force the closing.

If you put a clause in there that says the earnest money deposit will be sole and complete liquidated damages in case I decide I don't want to close, then you've already agreed what the damages are if you are in default of contract. The damages are measured by the amount of dollars you gave them as escrow money. That's all they get. The buyer can then walk away.

It's kind of like a "no personal liability real estate contract." That's what turns your contract into an option. You expand that clause by saying you can close on the contract anytime during the 12 months after the date you signed the real estate contract.

Some people like to be sneaky. They like to use a real estate contract and stick these clauses in there and never say the word "option."

LIQUIDATED DAMAGES: In the event purchaser defaults in the performance of this agreement, Seller shall retain the amount of the deposit, or three percent (3%) of the purchase price, whichever is lesser, as liquidated damages for such default. The remainder of the deposit, if any, shall be refunded to purchaser. The parties agree to confirm this provision upon making the additional deposit with the escrow holder. If you, as a seller, set the level of liquidated damages unreasonably high, courts might consider it to be a penalty and therefore refuse to enforce it.

So if I use a real estate contract I put the word OPTION in large clear type in front of REAL ESTATE CONTRACT to be sure there is no doubt about the fact that we're turning a real estate contract into an option. *A real estate contract is not an option without some kind of liquidated damage clause.* Remember it is important that all parties to a real estate contract clearly understand the terms of the transaction.

Remember, each state has its own forms. Some states have forms approved by the Realtors, some by the State Bar Association, some by the state and on it goes.

Option forms are less standard, but they are available.

These forms are provided here, not because they are great or even include all the special clauses I like. Not so. There are some non-standard clauses, but my "model" documents are at the back of the text.

But to give you something for reference, so you won't have to put the book down at this point and run to a stationery store, we inserted these samples.

Chapter One

Chapter Two

Sample Lease With Option

Perhaps the best way to move your option knowledge forward at this point would be to read several option forms. One is included here. The others are in the back of this text. This should help tie together what we have discussed and open new ideas and bring up questions we will cover later. We've included lease option formats too, in that most readers are used to them because they are commonly used. We'll refer back to them later in the Lease Options portion of the text.

Option Agreement

THIS AGREEMENT made and entered into this ___ day of _____, 19__ by and between _____ and all title holders to the property (hereinafter referred to as "SELLER"), and _____ (hereinafter referred to as "BUYER").

This Agreement is with respect to property commonly known as: _____ Street and legally described on attached Exhibit A, which is made a part hereof.

In consideration of the promises, the parties hereto agree as follows:

1.0 Consideration: In consideration of _____ dollars ($____) per month paid beginning _____, 19__ and other good and valuable consideration, SELLER grants to BUYER or assigns, an exclusive option to purchase the Property for the sum of _____ ($____) for the first ____ months from date of agreement and _____ ($__,____) thereafter.

1.1 Term of Option: Said option shall be exercised no sooner than_____ (__) months after date of option nor later than_____ (__) months after the commencement of said option term. The exercise of said Option shall be evidenced by delivery of a_____ (__) day written election to exercise fully executed by BUYER, and delivered to SELLER within the prescribed exercise period.

1.2 In the event of the exercise of said option, it is understood and agreed that if any rent payments are received by owner during the term of this option, said rent payments shall not be applied against the purchase price. Only the $_____ monthly option money referred to herein shall be applied to reduce the balance due seller in the event of exercise of option. In the event of a default of payments due under the option, all option payments (and/or any lease payments) will be forfeited and forever be the property of SELLER.

1.3 Loan Information: Attached to and made a part hereof is a schedule of loan(s) which are filed as a lien(s) against the Property at date of this agreement. BUYER may assume said loans at time of exercise of option should lender so permit, paying the balance due SELLER, (the difference between the loan(s) and option exercise price), in_____ (__) equal monthly amortized payments together with interest at ____ percent annual rate.

2. The prompt payment of the option payment is a major consideration in the owner's granting this option. Default shall be defined as option payments being made_____ (__) or more days late. Acceptance of any late option payment is an automatic waiver of default.

3. Exercise - Real Estate Contract: In the event of the exercise of said option, the sale of the property from SELLER to tenant shall be evidenced by a warranty deed and closed as per a standard form Real Estate Contract as officially adopted by local Realtors as set forth in Exhibit "B".

4. SELLER Has Title: SELLER represents that he has a bona fide contract in good standing or is in title to the Property and it is not now in default on any liens thereon. SELLER to provide BUYER proof of title and satisfactory loan status prior to this agreement's date of commencement or BUYER may void this agreement and any other agreement concerning BUYER, SELLER, and this property and all monies paid will be refunded buyer. Said proof to

Sample Lease With Option

be to the satisfaction of BUYER. In addition, SELLER agrees to immediately forward to BUYER a true and correct copy of any notice sent to him by any lender or the owner with respect to any defaults on this Property and where possible, approve lenders sending duplicate notices directly to buyer. A notice of "equitable interest" shall be signed and filed at signing of option.

5.0 All notices and payments required or permitted to be given to BUYER or SELLER hereunder shall be delivered as follows:

BUYER: SELLER:

_____   _____

_____   _____

5.1 Notice of change of address shall be given in writing.

6.0 Loan delinquent: Should SELLER be in delinquent on any payment due under the first note and mortgage outlined in the attached, or any other lien of record against the property on date of signing this option. BUYER may, at BUYER'S option, make such payment and receive____

dollars ($____) credit towards purchase of subject property for every $1.00 expended.

7.0 Loan default: Should SELLER cause any note and mortgage outlined in the attached listing of liens to be foreclosed upon, or notice of foreclosure filed, then BUYER may at his discretion cure the default and pay SELLER_____ dollars ($_____) for SELLER'S entire remaining equity as a full and complete purchase price to the seller and the difference that would have been due is waived as full and complete liquidated damages in that exact damages would be impossible if not difficult to calculate. The seller will execute a recordable general warranty deed as then specified and in so doing waive any and all redemptive rights.

8.0 SELLER shall not further encumber, nor do anything to permit any encumbrance, on this property during the term of this agreement.

9.0 During the term of this option SELLER shall insure the property against physical damage, casualty etc. for _____ DOLLARS ($____) for the first ____ (__) months and _____ ($____) thereafter plus additional amounts as indicated by property value increases.

BUYER will be named in the policy "as an additional insured, as his interest may appear."

IN WITNESS WHEREOF, the parties have signed this Agreement the day and year first above written.

by: _____ Date: SELLER(S)

by: _____ Date: BUYER(S)

Lease Agreement

THIS LEASE made this ____ day of _____ , 19__ by and between _____ as the owner of the Property located at _____ hereinafter referred to as the "Property", said owner hereinafter referred to as "Landlord", and _____ of _____ , _____ hereinafter referred to as "Tenant".

WITNESSETH:

Landlord hereby leases to Tenant (for occupancy and use as a private dwelling and storage of tenant's personal property, and no other purpose whatsoever except as allowed by_____ Zoning), creating a _____ (__) month tenancy, unless terminated as hereinafter provided, for the sum of _____ DOLLARS ($_____), beginning on the_____ day _____, 19__ , payable in equal monthly installments of_____ DOLLARS ($_____) each, to be in the office of Landlord IN ADVANCE OF the 1st day of each calendar month during the lease term.

Payments will be delivered or mailed to: _____

and if tenant chooses for any reason to be late, a late charge of _% will be imposed as of _ p.m. on the 15th of the month.

The parties hereto further agree as follows:

1. **Care of Premises:** Tenant has inspected the property and acknowledges it is in a good clean condition. Tenant shall take good care of the leased premises, fixtures and appurtenances thereto, and keep them in good repair, free from filth, overloading, danger of fire, explosion or nuisance, and return the same to Landlord at the expiration of the term, in as good condition as when received by Tenant, reasonable wear and use, damage by fire or other casualty not caused by negligence of Tenant, his family, guests or servants excepted. Tenant agrees to hold Landlord harmless from any liability arising from injury to person or property caused by any act or omission of Tenant, his family, guests, servants, assignees or subtenants.

2. **Alterations:** Tenant will not, without Landlord's written consent, make any major alterations in the leased premises and will not deface or permit the defacing of any part of the leased premises. Tenant shall comply with insurance regulations regarding fire, lightning, explosion, extended coverage and liability insurance; and nothing shall be done or kept in or on the premises by Tenant which will cause an increase on the premium for any such insurance on the premises or on any building of which the premises are a part or on any contents located therein over the rate usually obtained for the proper use of the premises permitted by this Lease or which will cause an increase of the premium for any such insurance on the premises or on any building of which the premises permitted by this Lease or which will cause cancellation of any such insurance; and Tenant further agrees to comply with all city ordinances and the laws of this state and to save Landlord harmless for or on account of all charges or damages for non-observance thereof.

3. Assigning or Subleasing: Tenant shall have the right to assign, transfer or encumber this Lease or any part thereof, with written notice to Landlord and shall have the right to sublet or allow any other tenant to come in with or under Tenant. The undersigned Tenant shall, however, remain personally liable for damage done by any such future tenants.
4. Rules: Tenant will observe and comply with such reasonable rules as Landlord may prescribe from time to time on written notice to Tenant for the safety, care and cleanliness of the property. A true and correct copy of the current rules if any, are attached.
5. Utilities: Tenant shall furnish and pay for all electricity, gas, fuel, and other services used in or assessed against the leased premises.
6. Damage by Casualty: In the event of damage to the leased premises by fire, explosion, providential means or any other casualty, without the fault of Tenant, and if the damage is so extensive that it cannot reasonably be repaired within thirty (30) days after the date of such damage, then at the option of tenant the term hereby created shall terminate as of the date of such damage and rent shall cease as of such date on the condition that Tenant forthwith surrenders the premises to Landlord. In all other cases where the leased premises are damaged by fire or other casualty without the fault of Tenant, Landlord shall have the option to terminate this Lease by giving written notice of his intention to do so within five (5) days after such casualty, or Landlord, at his option, may elect to repair the damage with reasonable dispatch, and if the damage has rendered the premises untenantable, in whole or in part, there shall be an apportionment of rent until the damage has been repaired. In case of such damage, whether this lease is terminated or not, Tenant shall remove all of the rubbish and debris of Tenant property within five (5) days after written request by Landlord and, if this Lease is not thereby terminated, Tenant shall not do anything to hinder or delay Landlord's work of repair and will cooperate with Landlord in such work. Landlord shall not be liable for inconvenience to Tenant by making repairs to any part of the premises or building, nor for the restoration of any improvements made by Tenant, nor for the restoration of any property of Tenant.
7. Eminent Domain. If the leased premises, or any part thereof, are taken by virtue of eminent domain, this Lease shall expire on the date when the same shall be so taken and return shall be apportioned as of said date. No part of any award for the leased premises, however, shall belong to Tenant.
8. Landlord's Liability. All merchandise and property in or about the leased premises shall be at Tenant's sole risk, and Tenant does hereby, now and forever, release Landlord from any claim for damages, howsoever caused. Landlord shall not be liable for damages or injury to any person occurring within the leased premises, unless proximity caused by or resulting from the negligence of Landlord, its agents, servants, or employees in the operation or maintenance of the leased premises.
9. Default. If (a) there be default in the payment of any rent when due and continuing for _____ (__) working days thereafter, or (b) there be default in any other of Tenant's obligations hereunder, and if any such default or condition, then in either such event, (a) or (b), Landlord may, at Landlord's option, at any time thereafter while such default or condition continues upon

proper legal process, declare this Lease terminated and enter upon and repossess the premises, as aforesaid. The Landlord then, as agent of Tenant, may relet the same for the balance of the term of this Lease, or for a shorter or longer term, and may receive the rents therefore, applying the same, first to the payment of the expenses of such reletting, including brokerage, cleaning, repairs, and decorations, and then to the payment of rent due and to become due by this Lease and performance of the other covenants of Tenant as herein provided; and Tenant agrees, whether or not Landlord has relet, to pay to Landlord the rent and other sums herein agreed to be paid by Tenant, less the net proceeds of the reletting, if any, as ascertained from time to time, and the same shall be payable by Tenant on the days above specified for the payment of rent. If any such default be other than for non-payment of money and it would take more than _____ (__) working days to cure the same, Landlord shall not terminate this Lease or enter upon the premises for such default if Tenant begins to cure such default within _____ (__) working days and proceeds with the cure therefore with due diligence to completion. Tenant shall pay to Landlord the amount of any reasonable legal or attorney's fees if Landlord must take legal action to compel performance by Tenant of his obligations hereunder or any legal action in connection with Tenant's tenancy hereunder.

10. **Fixtures.** All repairs, affixed improvements, alterations, additions, installations, permanently installed equipment and fixtures, by whomsoever installed or erected shall belong to Landlord and remain on and be surrendered with the leased premises as a part thereof at the expiration of this Lease.

11. **Waiver.** A waiver by Landlord of any default hereunder for a period of _____ (__) days shall be construed to be a continuing waiver of such default or breach, but not as a waiver or permission, express or implied, of any other or subsequent default or breach.

12. **Notices.** Any notice to Tenant required by law, lease or otherwise shall be sufficient if delivered to Tenant sent by first class mail, postage prepaid, to Tenant at the Property or at a post office box should tenant so designate in writing subsequent to signing this lease.
Any notice of intention to vacate, or any other notice from Tenant to Landlord, shall be in writing and delivered personally to Landlord or delivered to:_____ , Landlord's agent.

13. **Landlord's Right of Entry.** With _____ hour notice Landlord or Landlord's agent may enter the premises at reasonable hours to examine the same and to do anything which Landlord may deem necessary or advisable for the good of the premises or any building of which they are a part; and within one (1) month before the termination of this Lease, Landlord may display a "For Rent" sign on the premises and show same to prospective tenants. If Tenant(s) shall not be personally present to permit any such permissible entry into the premises, Landlord may enter same by a master key, without being liable in damages therefore and without affecting the obligations of Tenant hereunder.

14. **Representation.** Landlord has made no promise to alter, repair, decorate or improve the premises, but represents the condition and repair of the premises to be in good workable order, except as are set forth herein. Neither party has made any representation or promises, except as contained herein. Tenant liability for rent shall not commence until possession is given or the leased premises are available for occupancy by Tenant. No such failure to give possession shall in anyway affect the validity of this lease. Lack of notice to Landlord of needed repairs within __ days of

Tenant's entry into possession of the leased premises shall be conclusive evidence that the lease premises and the building of which it is a part are in good and satisfactory order and repair at such time.

15. Successors. The provisions, covenants and conditions of this Lease shall bind and inure to the benefit of the heirs, legal representatives, successors and assigns for each of the parties hereto, except that no assignment, encumbrance or subletting by Tenant without written consent of Landlord shall vest any right in the assignee, encumbrancer or sublessee of Tenant. Landlord shall be released from and Landlord's grantee shall be liable for, all liability of Landlord hereunder accruing from and after such grant of the revision.

16. As a material inducement to Tenant to perform under the term of this lease in a prompt manner, without delays whatsoever, Tenant will be given an option to purchase subject property. During the first _____ (__) months of occupancy, should tenant be in default of any payment due longer than thirty (30) days, in addition to the normal remedies under this Lease, the option will be null and void forevermore, and Landlord will keep all rent and all option consideration as full liquidated damages for all claims (except the cost of physical damage to the property) in that actual damages would be difficult if not impossible to ascertain, and all parties will hold each other harmless.

_____
LANDLORD

_____
TENANT

The agreements you have just reviewed, (including those in the back of the book) are meant as samples. They are available from the various publishers listed on each document. Please contact them. You should not assume that any single option form is right for all situations — or for any particular situation. Read them all carefully, they all have their strengths and weaknesses. (You may end up picking one that fits you or selecting various parts of each to use.)

As an example, in a real estate contract turned into an option, you cover the need for title policies, insurance, notes evidenced by mortgages and deeds of trust and so on and so forth, all outlined. You have the legal description, price all laid out. But it isn't easy to use with complex formats like equity share lease options as we will cover later.

Even when I use a formal OPTION AGREEMENT I will add a clause at the end saying: when it comes time to close, we will close as per the standard clauses in the attached real estate contract. That's because most option agreements do a poor job of explaining how you close. You always need to make sure the steps to close are clear. That's all. Clear and complete.

So study all the forms and pick what fits or draw from the best part of each. Just think through your selection.

Referring to paragraph 2 of the Option Agreement, while many sellers may not accept the time payment approach on an option, enough sellers do--so it is worth requesting.

Re-read paragraphs 6 & 7 of the Option Agreement. Penalties of any sort must meet the criteria of reasonableness. If they exceed an accepted definition of what courts deem reasonable, they may be considered punitive in nature and not be enforceable. On the other hand these terms may make the seller more careful than he or she might otherwise have been.

State requirements vary considerably, they may change frequently and are often confusing. Because contracts are legal documents it is strongly suggested you have all agreements, both standard and non-standard, reviewed by competent local legal advisors.

Chapter Two

Chapter Three

How To Write Option Contracts

What Option Form Should I Use?

We have provided you with several forms in this text. We have also shown how to modify a real estate contract to make it an option (at the back of this book) and given you ideas on how to write your own. But remember, **STATE LAW GOVERNS OPTIONS.** You'll therefore need to check the laws of the state in which the property is located.

If you are just studying and not ready to write an offer, office supply and/or printing shops supply "legal forms" for less than $1 per form. You may also go to your local library and ask for a real estate forms book.

Many of the agreements in this book could be used without change IN MOST STATES. They were drawn from my transactions in Colorado, Kansas, Missouri, Texas and California.

We don't warrant their applicability in any given state. So, as we always advise, to be safe - a good REAL ESTATE LAWYER should review any documents, options or any papers that have not been reviewed for legality in your state. Get a quote of how much he or she will charge.

Filling Out The Forms

In filling out the option portion of a lease option, several factors must be observed. They can be summarized with two important words - clarity and completeness.

First, *is the lease option all in one document?* If it is, it's simpler. If not, read even more carefully.

Address:

If all is in one document, then it will suffice to state the commonly known or street address and legal description one time. If you use two documents, it would be smart to repeat these key items in both the lease and the option.

If there are two documents, a lease and an option, the option and lease CAN be tied together. A clause such as the one that follows is common:

> *"This option is a part of a lease of even date concerning the subject property and by reference hereto is made a part hereof."*

Because some options and leases are drawn at the same time, but are not legally tied together, make sure that **both** documents repeat the information necessary to identify the property.

Expiration date:

All contracts with expiration dates should be as precise as possible. Since an option holder could potentially lose many valuable rights at the expiration of the option, clarity is important here too. *Here's a good example:*

> *"This option shall expire at noon, July 18, 1989."*

Here's a bad example:

> *"The purchase rights contained herein expire 36 months after close of option unless extended."*

Does it expire on the first day or last day of the 36th month? When was the "close of option?"

Another example is "unless extended." This could be a perpetual right to continue the option. I've seen them all.

Attorneys refer to such poorly written clauses as "litigation language." This means that no two people representing each party would be able to agree on what the clause really meant. The interpretation may have to come as a result of a lawsuit.

Time of Exercise:

Many options can be exercised anytime prior to the expiration date. If this is the case, say so. If not, be clear when the option may be exercised.

EXAMPLE: You give someone an option on your farm on May 15, 1986. The option is for 36 months, but you want the use of the land until the end of

1986. Here is what you could include in your option: "This option cannot be exercised prior to January 1, 1987."

The prohibition against exercise is also a common technique to make sure the seller doesn't have a taxable event, (closed sale), until a future tax year.

Price and option money:

MOST ERRORS OCCUR when spelling out a creative pricing formula. Here's a correct and simple plan.

> *"The purchase price will be $100,000, with the $10,000 paid herein as option consideration applying to reduce the amount due seller at time of exercise to $90,000."*

Here's the WRONG way to say the same thing!

> *"The $10,000 option money is to be applied to the price." (Who knows what that means? I'm sure the seller would say you owe $110,000!)*

If you want the price to go up, rather than state a formula, **it is safer to state the dollar amounts.** In fact, it's safest to state *both*.

> *"The purchase price shall be increased 10% annually, as per the table below: If purchased between The price will be:"*
>
> | If purchased between | The price will be: |
> |---|---|
> | Jan. 1, 1988 and noon Dec. 31, 1988 | $100,000.00 |
> | Jan. 1, 1989 and noon Dec. 31, 1989 | $110,000.00 |
> | Jan. 1, 1990 and noon Dec. 31, 1990 | $121,000.00 |
> | Jan. 1, 1991 and noon Dec. 31, 1991 | $133,000.00 |

Other problems come up when you state that the "price," (which you've failed to define properly earlier), will be increased at the end of an ambiguous time period, (like "300 days after option holder is *moved in*), and increased by a questionable index, such as an amount equal to the increase in rents for the area."

Chapter Three

Parties:

All contracts suffer when the parties to the contact are not clearly defined. It's easy to make things complicated. For instance, Mr. Owner is the seller of the option, the optionor and the seller of the property later on. On top of that, he could be "the party of the first part!"

Form contracts do help because they are usually consistent. Mr. Owner is called one name consistently throughout. But be careful to use the same terms when you add clauses or exhibits or such.

In custom-drawn documents be sure to be consistent. If in the first paragraph you state, "Mr. Owner, known herein as the property holder and optionor," don't start mentioning a "seller." Throughout this text we have suggested a great many creative, innovative approaches to real estate. The very nature of these concepts renders them "non-standard" --otherwise they would not be innovative. It is important therefore, that you obtain competent local legal advice as you implement your way to success.

The lease portion:

The primary precaution in filling out the lease portion of a lease option relates to option credits and joint default. **These two topics could be covered in the lease or in the option portion. Just to be clear.**

Credits:

If the rent is applied to reduce what is due at the time of purchase, state that fact and make sure to repeat it! Your lease might state:

> *"Two-hundred dollars ($200) per month of the rent paid will be credited as option consideration and will be applied to reduce the purchase price at time of exercise."*

And in the option under the section dealing with price:

> *"—less additional option consideration of $200 per month, paid as a part of rent, as per paragraph 12 of the lease agreement attached hereto and of even date."*

If your option is to purchase a property with the intent of development, MAKE SURE YOUR OPTION GIVES YOU THE RIGHT TO PROCEED WITH DEVELOPMENT WHILE THE PROPERTY IS UNDER OPTION.

As a primary concern, you may want to apply for zoning. This can be a complicated area.

Most zoning commissions today want you to present potential development plans as a part of zoning approval. Gone are the days when you could simply ask for 17 acres to be zoned maximum density "apartments," with no specific development plans.

Prior to the mid-1970s, this was done frequently, just to up the value of land for resale. Since then, city and county planning committees have become very population and land-use conscious. They see their job as controlling and directing growth, not "aiding" the net worth of land speculators.

A knowledgeable land owner might not agree to allow you to proceed with development plan approval. If you get the land planned and zoned and don't buy it, the landowner may be stuck with your unexecuted plans for years and years to come.

Besides, most savvy zoning boards won't allow anyone but the land title holder to submit a proposal.

A broad power right might say, "Optionee shall have the right to seek and obtain rezoning approval from R-1 to R-8. Optionor will cooperate and assist as required, including but not limited to signing all zoning applications and all other documents required for various private and government zoning groups."

Of course, you do run the risk of alerting owners to the possibilities of new uses of their property. However, our research indicates most owners who have decided to sell an option on their property have based this decision on a variety of personal factors, and may be aware of other uses, but take action for a myriad of personal reasons.

Asking questions of the seller should tell you their level of knowledge as to other uses for the property. Ask questions first!

The same would hold true for FIX UP. Not all sellers would allow you to tear out a kitchen you are "going" to replace. Wouldn't it be a shame to get it out only to have the seller discover your mess and sue you? If you had the right to rehab during the option period written into the option, there would be no doubt to your right to do so. And, as you negotiate for that permission, any fears the seller might have could be dealt with beforehand.

The lease option need not be drawn properly unless one of these items are important to you:

AS AN OWNER

1. You want to receive the rent on time and hassle free.

2. You don't like being sued.

Chapter Three

AS A TENANT/OPTION HOLDER

1. You really think the property will be worth more than your option price some day.

2. You don't like being sued.

Remember, business runs smoothly when you do your homework. Lease options can be complex. Even "simple" lease options on rental houses leave room for error. Simple "standard forms" help, but changes, additions, and modifications all leave room for error.

Is hiring a good lawyer the best way to protect your legal interests? You bet it is. As you progress as a new professional investor you will have more and more to contribute to the structuring of your deals. Becoming rich is a do-it-yourself business--and you will want competent legal advice from an attorney specializing in real estate, all along the way. Be sure to talk with experienced, successful investors, brokers, CPA's and law school deans for their recommendations--the final selection of advisors is up to you.

The biggest mess I've witnessed was a case where the owner added the following words at the bottom of the house lease: "Tenant has the option to buy this house for $70,000." That's all! Talk about lawsuit potential. He was sure the option expired with the lease. Are you?

Does The Option Money Apply?

A $15,000 SEMINAR!

One of the items to cover and clarify is, "Does the option money apply?"

Over 15 years ago, I put a group of investors into an option. The lawyer, who used to office in Crown Center in Kansas City, did such a lousy job of drawing the documents that I could see when it got time to close that there was some question as to whether or not the $30,000 of option money applied toward the purchase price mentioned in the contract. I ended up having $15,000 of my own money in the deal and my investors had put in another $15,000. They got theirs out and I lost mine. (I didn't provide you with a copy of this option, dear reader, for fear you'd use it! It was 36 pages long and really *looked* good. It was just *so* long it started to contradict itself!)

I've learned that lesson the hard way. Just make sure the option is clear. "I give you $15,000 as option money. The purchase price is $100,000. That means at closing I owe you $85,000." Or you could say, "I give you $15,000 as option money. The purchase price is $100,000 and at closing I owe you $100,000 because the option money does not apply." However you negotiate the deal, it doesn't change the taxes. It doesn't change anything except how much you pay for the property, which is sort of important, isn't it?

Prohibition Against Future Borrowing

Let me go back to a point we discussed earlier. I have an option on your property. Within that option I say as part of the option consideration you agree that you won't borrow any more money against the property without my permission. *That's a prohibition against future borrowing.*

While the prohibition on borrowing restrictions on the owner may be a negative to the owner, we feel it is an important protection for the buyer--optionee. Recording your option makes conventional re-financing close to impossible--but it is safest if you also prohibit it in the agreement itself. If you record your "Notice of Option" this prohibition being written in the document becomes a negotiable item.

If there's a first mortgage, the next thing recorded will be my notice of option. Legally, technically, if I have a recorded option, (or notice of option), against your property, nobody can record a second without their second being behind or subordinate to my option.

I don't even *have* to tell you that there is a prohibition against future borrowing because most likely no lender would ever give you a loan once my option is recorded. I just want to put that clause in as an extra safeguard. I don't want there to be any doubt.

So, if I make it perfectly clear in the filed, recorded notice of option that there's a prohibition against future borrowing, then no one can go into court and claim anything other than the fact that his note was in violation of a previous contractual agreement. We had full, complete consideration.

A Preliminary Option Agreement

The option contract itself need not be lengthy or involved. It should be signed by all parties. You give them the money for the option consideration at the time of closing. That's sometimes called the first closing or the closing of the option to separate it from the closing when you receive the deed to the property.

I quite often write a preliminary option agreement. The first closing is when I give them the money on the option. The second closing is if I buy the option on the property. In that PRELIMINARY OPTION AGREEMENT I am going to say that when I give them the option money they are going to give me all documents that have to do with protection against foreclosure and protecting my other rights, including a signed and notarized NOTICE OF OPTION.

What Is A Notice Of Option?

When I hold an option on a piece of property I don't want anybody to know my terms, my way of buying that property. It's none of their business! I have to protect myself. I NEVER record my option documents because that tells too much. But I want something of record to protect my position.

EXAMPLE: Louise wants to buy my property. I want $500,000 for it. She says she will tell me in a day or so whether she will take it or not. So Louise meets with Christine and tells her, "I'm thinking about buying Barney's

Chapter Three

Notice Of Option

Be the world hereby apprised that Bernard Hale Zick DBA Zick Investment Properties, optionee, P.O. Box 630, Solana Beach, CA 92075 has an option to purchase the following legally described property:

Lot 2, Block 7, Sherwood Forest, Nottingham County, VA

The option agreement is of an even date. Anybody deal- dealing in and with the subject property should contact the optionee at P O Box 630, Solana Beach, CA 92075.

IN WITNESS WHEREOF, the parties have signed this agreement.

by: _____ Date:05/13/86
    Property owner(optionor)

by: _____ Date:05/13/86
    Optionee

STATE OF _____

COUNTY OF _____

On this _____ day of _____ , _____ , _____ before me, a Notary Public, personally appeared _____ and _____ who executed the above and foregoing instrument their _____ and acknowledged that they executed the same as their free act and deed. In WITNESS WHEREOF, I have hereunto set my hand and affixed my seal the day and year first above written.

Notary Public

MY COMMISSION EXPIRES:

Notice Of Option

Be the world hereby apprised that _____
_____ optionee has an option to
purchase the following legally described property:

The option agreement is of an even date. Anybody deal- dealing in and with
the subject property should contact optionee at:_____
_____

IN WITNESS WHEREOF, the parties have signed this agreement.

by: _____ Date:05/13/86
    Property owner(optionor)
by: _____ Date:05/13/86
    Optionee

STATE OF _____

COUNTY OF _____

On this _____ day of _____ ,
_____, _____ before me, a
Notary Public, personally appeared _____ and
_____ who executed the above and foregoing
instrument their _____ and acknowledged that they executed the
same as their free act and deed. In WITNESS WHEREOF, I have hereunto
set my hand and affixed my seal the day and year first above written.

Notary Public

MY COMMISSION EXPIRES:

property for $500,000. Think it's worth it?" Christine says, "Oh, sure. Boy, will Barney be glad to sell that property!"

Louise wants to know why and Christine says she was down at the courthouse looking at county records the other day and happened to look up information about that property, as she was interested in it herself. She saw that Barney had an option to buy that property for $100,000 and the option was to expire next July 14. "If you don't buy that property from him, he not only won't make $400,000 in profit — I know Barney can't get the $100,000 together to buy that property and he'll lose the entire option!"

So Louise gives me a call the next day. Sweet, wonderful Louise. She says, "Barney, about that property. I do want to buy it and I'll give you $110,000 but not $500,000."

That's the reason I NEVER RECORD MY OPTION. It contains too much personal information in there. **I DO RECORD A NOTICE OF OPTION.**

See completed example and blank form for your use on following two pages. (**NOTE:** "of even date" means that the Notice of Option was signed on the same day that the Option was signed.)

I might even want to put a paragraph in that document that says, "the option agreement itself contains a prohibition against future borrowing," if I happen to have negotiated this into the transaction. But, I'm not going to tell the world about the price or terms.

If you were concerned about telling the world that you've entered an *option*, then use the words, "an agreement concerning the subject property."

As a variation, I once made a notice of option by using white paper or correction tape to cover up the terms and conditions of buying that were written into the option. I photocopied the whole thing, drew a line through the white space and at the top where it said OPTION I typed "Notice Of." The guy signed the second copy and I filed that. Thus, everything was filed and of record - except the price and terms.

I took the modified option to be recorded as a notice of option with me for signature at the same time I took the option to be signed.

Securing Your Option

An excellent way of securing your option or notice of option is to record it with a deed of trust or mortgage. That way you can foreclose on the owner if he doesn't make payments on his first and is therefore in default under the option agreement. **An option and a notice of option don't carry a lot of weight - BUT A DEED OF TRUST DOES.**

While some owners may balk at providing a deed of trust or mortgage as security for an option, many will not. This extra degree of protection is well

How To Write Option Contracts

worth asking for. In the event the owner refuses such protection, you need to wonder why the owner objects. The Deed of Trust is a powerful document and is difficult to remove from a property without permission.

I am not going to spend a lot of time repeating this simple idea, but believe me, this one technique could well be the one most important idea in this entire book!

Recording gives public notice, optionee protection and the right to foreclose if the optionor is in default.

All you need is a standard form Deed of Trust or Mortgage. In the section that states, "This Deed of Trust is to secure a note (s) as follows" just add : "an option agreement with a value in excess of $ _____."

If you are worried about due on sale, leave out the word "option." Just say "an agreement..." The value is the dollar value of the equity today.

Most states require that both optionor and optionee have their signatures notarized for the notice of option to be recorded. I have had luck twice, getting a half signed notice recorded in the Miscellaneous Documents section, when all else failed.

It's been my experience that a valid option or notice of option will protect you if the IRS later files a tax lien against the owner of record. If filed, the IRS can seize the net proceeds from sale, (proceeds the optionor will receive from your purchase), but not lay claim to any value above the option price.

Length Of Option

The option will run until the two of you decide to cut it off. You should have a determinable time. It could be a day or 99 years.

When do you exercise the option? Whenever the two of you agree. You would assume a two-year option is exercised anytime during the two years. Not particularly so.

EXAMPLE: You are a teacher and I want an option to buy your house. You say that's fine but you don't want me to buy it during the school year. And after further consideration you decide you don't want to give me to option to buy at all!

I counter with an offer an option to buy your house during the next four years but I promise it will only be exercised in the months of June, July or August. That way you know you will be moved out of your house ONLY during those months of the year.

This procedure has worked well with farms, because the exercise period would not conflict with the dates when crops come in.

Chapter Three

There are many other alternatives dealing with the exercise period. If you want to make it hard for someone to exercise the option, make the exercise period short. A 13-month option could be exercisable only in the 13th month.

If you want to get nasty, you could make it the 56th week. Or, the day after the anniversary date, between 10 o'clock and 11 o'clock in the morning. The smaller the exercise option period, the less desirable the option is to the option holder. The longer and broader the period, the more power you have in your hand.

EXAMPLE: I have a 10-year option to buy a piece of property at a flat price. The price stays the same for 10 years. It's been five years now. It's quite a bit of land. I got a call from the owner of the property and he wanted to know if I was going to exercise that option. He said he could use a little cash. I told him I was not going to exercise at that time.

But I'll probably exercise that option 9 1/2 years after I signed it. Why? Because *an option is a form of interest free holding.* I get all the appreciation and don't have to pay interest nor taxes nor any holding costs until I exercise the option. (With an income property, there would be additional considerations.)

Notice Of Intent To Exercise

If I'm going to sell an option to someone, I want them to give me a notice of their intent to exercise the option. Thirty (30) days prior to the time they intend to exercise the option, they must give me written notice, by certified mail, of their intent to exercise. That is written into the option document.

Why? Because I don't want to get down to the last day, have the phone ring and hear somebody say, "Hello, I want to exercise my option now." Legally I have to exercise the option right then and there or I have to give him an extension, which is a very bad thing to do with an option.

Example Of Intent To Exercise

Dear _____ ,

RE: Notice of Intent to Exercise Option

This letter shall serve as written notice of my intent to exercise the option I hold on your property at (commonly known address) as per the option dated _____ , a copy of which is attached.

Signed,

Optionee

X_____

Chapter Three

Since timing can be a crucial variable in so many real estate transactions, it is suggested that the phrase "time is of the essence" be included in all options and extension clauses.

So, as a seller, you want a 30-day notice of intent to exercise the option. That puts you "on notice" - so you can get the paperwork done, research the title, order a title policy and such as that.

In some states it may be better to say you, as seller, want the buyer-optionee to notify you when he or she shall exercise the option, rather than he or she just intends to exercise the option. Check for the most appropriate legal language in your state.

Also, it isn't smart to be put in a situation where you have to extend a closing past the original date of expiration. Then you're in "never never land" because you have allowed the expiration date to go by and left the option open. **Your delay gives them an excuse to delay.** You have little leverage to force the buyer to complete the purchase.

As a buyer or option holder, you'd rather not be *required* to give notice. You'll have to make up your mind that many days sooner. But in either case, required or not, it is smart to let the seller know as soon as possible.

Briefly, the option agreement should be very specific. Lay out all the terms, telling you how to exercise it, how you pay for it. Put the terms in there. "At the time I exercise the option I give you (so many dollars down) and you carry back a note and the note will have terms and conditions as per the attached exhibit A."

To make everything *perfectly* clear, you can draw up the actual note you are going to use when you buy the property. Make this a part of the option for clarity.

Remember, you don't have to buy at full cash. You can include terms when you fund on the option. And, if you're going to use part cash and part owner carry back financing, or just all owner carry back, you eliminate so many potential arguments by presenting the note form you intend to use as part of the option.

Revoking Notice Of Intent

Once you send your notice of intent to exercise, legally you are bound to a two-way contractual agreement. It is no longer a unilateral situation.

Originally, with the option, they *had* to sell, you could decide to buy or not to buy. Once notice of intent to exercise is given, it's now a bilateral contract. **You've agreed to buy.**

So technically, if you give a notice of intent and then change your mind, you could be sued to complete the sale. That's called "specific performance," the applicable statutes may vary in each state.

Chapter Three

However, here is a real life example. A lawsuit isn't very likely.

EXAMPLE: A student gave me a call. His option was about to expire. The option price was $120,000 and the house was valued currently at $180,000. He *hoped* he could find a loan or a partner in the 35 days left on the option, but he wasn't sure. He didn't want to be sued.

I couldn't help but admonish him for waiting until the last minute to deal with the problem, but after I shook my finger, I offered this non-legal advise.

If you give notice and you raise the money, you have a great deal. If you fail to raise the money, you probably won't be sued. If they did, it would be suing to force you to buy a $180,000 property for $120,000! Mind you, the $180,000 was a solid value and **the sellers didn't want the option to be exercised.**

And if he *was* sued, what a deal! Such a suit would last six months to two years. If the optionor/seller wins, all you've lost is legal fees, ($10,000 - $15,000) and you still get to buy for $120,000.

Don't get me wrong. This isn't normal advice and I'm not a lawyer. But it is something to consider if you are ever in the same situation. THIS SHOWS JUST HOW MUCH CONTROL AN OPTION GIVES YOU!

Informal Options

I know a lady who for $10 had 10 options on about $35 million worth of property. She had the options for a number of years. During all this time she had been working on the properties, trying to build a regional shopping center.

This lady took my "Creative Formulas Course" — in the late '70s. It was just called "Creative Real Estate" then. We used to do the seminar in three days, during the week, with property marketing on the third day. Most of the participants were brokers.

On the third day, this lady presented $35,000,000 worth of land she had under option. The questions flew hot and heavy. She didn't do a good job of defending her position. She either lacked formal control or just plain didn't know what she was doing.

A month or two after the seminar she hired me to come to her town for a day of counseling. (I do that now and then, but this trip was almost worth it to fulfill my curiosity - let alone the fee!)

My worst fears were realized. But at the same time, I was amazed.

A. The land was super! Each piece had a story and real potential. One piece wrapped around an existing shopping center!

B. **The lady didn't have a single option in writing.** "What!" you say. "Then she didn't really have an option."

Chapter Three

C. Not quite so. This lady had such control over the sellers, that several of those verbal agreements would be enforced. Not enforceable in court, but they would be enforced because the sellers felt bound to her.

I don't know if it was her "sweet grandmother" personality or her persistence - but some of these "deals" had been dragging on for nearly 10 years, with only $1 and a handshake.

After I give people my best advice, I usually try to get them additional help. Because nothing was in writing, I couldn't get any of the financially strong developers I knew to look at the property.

The lesson? **Verbal options are not recommended procedure.** I can't blame my developer friends, but I don't think I'd ever approve, (or even work on), an informal option.

There is a second lesson. The control of having the seller WANT you to exercise your option can go a long way. Now, if you can get that kind of psychological control - together with a properly written and legally enforceable option - THAT IS SOMETHING.

Since verbal agreements are subject to so much dispute and because only written agreements concerning real estate are enforceable under state Statutes of Fraud laws, it is essential that all terms and conditions of any contract or agreement be put in writing and be signed by all appropriate parties.

Chapter Three

Chapter Three

Chapter Four

Paying For Options

How Much Do You Pay For An Option?

If I'm buying one, less is better. If I'm selling, more is better. I've paid one dollar for several very valuable options. Why did the seller accept so little money? Because I told the person who owned the property - "How would you like to have a silent salesman? Let's pick the price that you know you'll be happy with any time during the next three years. If I can sell the property for more, you still get your full price. No fuss. No negotiations. I just write you a check."

From a contract law point of view, you really should say "one dollar and other valuable considerations." In fact, I usually reach in my pocket and pull out a green $1 bill and put it in their hands. Then if we ever go to court we can say that Bernard Zick actually handed you a green dollar bill, didn't he? (Now if we get up to $10, sometimes I get a little chintzy — just kidding!)

A dollar and other valuable considerations works quite well. You can say you'll pay $1 for the option because of all the work you must do. **But be careful.** If you say what specific things you are going to do and then you fail to perform, you could lose your option. If you specifically say you will rezone the property and the zoning board turns you down, you could be out of luck. If you say you'll clean and maintain the property, someone will have to **judge** just how good a job you did.

This relates to what we said earlier. BE CLEAR. If it is unclear as to when or if you have paid the option consideration, you lose.

EXAMPLE: You're interested in development land. If you state that you "will do a land plan," that is too vague. You have a defined consideration if you declare the following: "I will have a registered architect complete a land-use proposal consisting of a single site plan layout, a copy of which will be given to optionor within 90 days of the signing of this agreement."

Don't get funny and write the option for a consideration of $4.74. I tried that one time and my lawyer told me that for years attorneys have gone to court with option cases. He said there are countless cases proving a dollar is valuable consideration. "We don't know if $4.74 is valuable consideration and we'd have to prove it all over again in court." I know that sounds silly, but I took his advice. *So just say a dollar and other valuable consideration.*

WARNING: Some state courts have deemed options to be without consideration because $1 was not enough. I guess the potential option holder failed to show that there was any other "good and valuable consideration."

My Florida friends tell me they pay at least $100 and try to prove that more was included! In Florida they may tell you that you only have a partially executed contract. **Check your state laws and court cases.**

If a court would ever decide that the optionee hadn't given sufficient consideration, then the optionor or seller could "withdraw the offer to sell" and sell at will to another.

How Is It Paid?

I've paid cash or given property, but I always WANT TO BE ABLE TO PROVE THAT I'VE PAID. I have given the person a check which they immediately endorsed back to me and then I gave them the cash for it. A check from you to them, endorsed on the back is more impressive and easier to produce in court than a witness.

I've really never had any problem with proving payment. I've only had one argument over options and I've had about 80 different options in the last 14 years. That was one case where there was an argument over whether the option money was in addition to or subtracted from the selling price. I've never had somebody argue whether or not they gave suitable consideration.

Just make sure the consideration is both clear and sufficient. Even though anything will serve as consideration, you don't want to argue the point later in court.

While courts do not ordinarily try to determine the correct amount of consideration agreed upon, they may judge if the consideration has value and if the consideration was actually given.

If, on the other hand, the consideration is judged to be less than adequate (a sign of insincerity) then it may contribute to the appearance of deception or fraud by the optionee.

On occasion, if a deal is perceived by the courts as "too good a deal" (a subjective judgment at best), obtaining a specific performance remedy may prove difficult. You can see the importance of creating a transaction which satisfies the requirements of both parties--it is less likely to precipitate legal action.

Chapter Four

Paying For Options

You Can Use Anything To Pay For An Option

How much and what do you have to pay for an option? It's whatever you agree on. One of my favorite examples concerns a farmer and his farm.

EXAMPLE: You are seeking an option to buy this farm. You say, "Mr. Farmer, can I have an option on your property?" He says he wants to keep farming it for the next five years. You tell him you'll take an option on the farm. The option is good in the fifth year and that way he can farm for five more years and you can buy it only after that.

The farmer says, "That's fine and dandy, but I don't need to pay any more taxes, I don't want any more money."

"No, Mr. Farmer. If I give you this money it is not taxable to you for five years because the option cannot be exercised or can't expire for five years. Therefore, you are taxed on the money after it is time to retire. It will be part of the purchase price or you will pay taxes on it if the option is allowed to expire and is not exercised." (See Chapter Nine on taxes.)

The farmer said, sorry, he doesn't like new fangled ideas.

Not to be discouraged, you go into town to the John Deere dealer. You have him load up a brand new green combine and take it out to the farm. You have the farmer get into the combine and drive it around - the combine with the big air conditioned cab and the 8- track tape player. You slip in a Dolly Parton tape. The farmer falls in love with the combine.

You say, *"Mr. Farmer, you can use this combine for the next five years to farm your land if you'll give me an option to buy the farm in the fifth year."*

The farmer just loves the combine and says YES! You have leased the tractor, so your money is not tied up. Since it is a financing lease, you can write off the interest on the lease AND get investment tax credit on the combine. At the end of five years you get the tractor/combine back and, if history is any proof of the future, it will probably be worth more than what you paid for it. (In this particular example at this particular time I also owned the leasing company so I got the profit on financing the lease.)

As time goes by, an expressway cuts through the farm and you now own pre-development land.

The farmer uses the cash to buy a larger farm or retires. As you can see—you can use anything to pay for an option!

EXAMPLE: I know of a person who actually got a beautiful little sports car and went over to a man's house, knocked on the door and said to his wife, (because he could never get the man to do a deal with him), "Do you like that car?"

Chapter Four

She said yes and he told her to use it for the day. If she liked it, she could have it, IF she got her husband to sign this document. The document was an option to buy a very prime piece of land that the man owned. You know he got the option.

Vacant lots bought at tax sales, recreational lots, purchased in a weak moment on a "free" trip to a resort, time shares, gemstones, jewelry, cars, boats, antiques, and services can be used as option consideration—not to mention, second mortgages, personal notes, accounts receivable and notes you draw up and either secure with real estate, personal property or use unsecured.

Four Ways To Set The Price

There are four basic ways to set your final purchase price. Some contracts will call the price the "striking price" or the "option price" or the "exercise price" or the "price at time of second closing".

The last approach is used by option contract drafters when they first write a contract between the optionee and optionor. When that contract is signed and money (for the option) changes hands, that's called the first closing. Later, when the property changes hands, it's called "the second closing".

Here are the four:

1. A price for the property, with increases as time goes by.

2. A price for the property that is fixed.

3. A price for the equity that increases as time goes by.

4. A price for the equity that is fixed.

Now, remember it doesn't make any difference whether it is written up that the option money is in addition to or part of the option price. You can pay $10,000 for the right to get the property for an additional $90,000. Or you could pay $10,000 for the option to buy the property for $100,000 *and the option money applies to the purchase price.* The tax effects are the same, the total paid, in this case, is the same. Just be clear that you underline the fact that the option money applies so the seller doesn't say you owe $110,000 in total!

The $100,000 price could be good for one year. If the option is not exercised within that year, the option price would increase. The increase could be a fixed percentage, say 10%, and be good for one more year. That would mean you'd pay $110,000 in year two. If the option lasted longer, say three years, the price would be $121,000 the next, or third, year.

The increase for the property could be calculated by some formula. The increase for year two could be equal to the percentage increase in the consumer price index. Or if it were a farm under option, you might use a farm land index.

Paying For Options

It would make sense to me if the index used related to the property and the closer, the better. But, I've seen increases based on all sorts of things. One seller wanted the money now, no options. He wanted to invest in a specific stock. He argued that if he were to give an option, the exercise price would have to increase each six months by the amount that the stock increased!

Inflation isn't a sure thing. If you agree to a rate of increase that exceeds the rate of value growth in the property, you'll have no profit in your option. That might be okay if your only reason for getting the option was to keep others from buying, but most options are for profit.

An owner experiencing a high vacancy factor and excessive turnover may be willing to grant a renewing tenant an option to buy as a condition of renewal.

A fixed price option is better, because the option holder gets all value increases.

I've allowed sellers the first type of option price, but it usually wasn't very profitable. Letting the option price go up a fixed percentage makes sense and it could be a protective back door.

Let me explain. Let's say you really only need a year in which to exercise the option. But you don't want to cut your timing that tight. A potential second year at $110,000 is better than only one year at $100,000. If very high expectations of gain are on the horizon, the price increasing method might be justified.

EXAMPLE: The 10 acre "farm" isn't even worth $100,000 - more like $90 - $95,000. The odds of it hitting $110,000 in 13 months under normal circumstances are less than slim. But your cousin works for Ford and he just came to town to quietly close on a new plant site. The corner of the plant will be 1,000 yards from the farm. If the plant goes, the land is worth $250 - $350,000.

Table A

Equity increased at 10% annually

$20,000.00 compounded = $32,210.20 equity
                       + 60,000.00 loan
                       _____
Option price in last year $92,210.20

Total price increased at 10% annually

$80,000 compounded = $128,840.80

In general, whether the option term is short or long, a fixed price option is better. It just makes sense — there is less risk with a fixed price.

An option to purchase a

Chapter Four

Chart   **5 years**

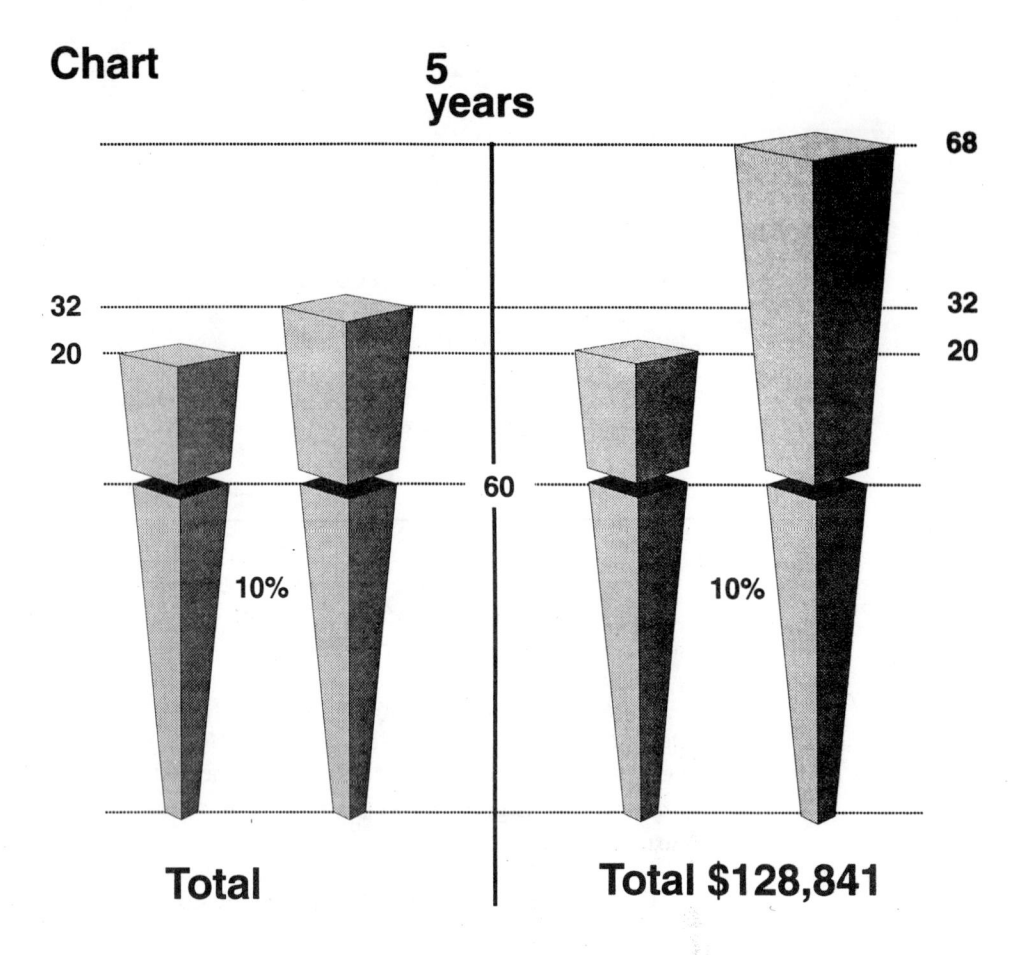

(Bar chart showing: Left side "Total" with bars at 20 and 32 with 10%; Right side "Total $128,841" with bars at 20 and 68 with 10%; center line marked 60)

property for an increasing price for the equity is even better.

EXAMPLE: The seller wants to sell for $80,000 and his equity is $20,000. He says he'll give you the five year option you want, but he won't go for a flat price. Since he'd only get $20,000 cash if you paid in full, you agree to give him a 10% annual increase on the equity.

Look at the difference. $20,000 increased at 10% a year for 5 years would be $32,210.20. This is a much cheaper price than $80,000, increased by (10%) per year which would total $128,841.00 at the end of five years.

By having the increase set on only a portion of the value, (the equity), the property need not perform nearly as well to be profitable. Remember, our $80,000 starting price?

A deal struck on a 10% increase in the equity per year would have to have the total property appreciate at a much slower overall annual rate, than a deal done at 10% IN CREASE IN TOTAL PRICE for the property. In this case, the first property, the one that had its price figured on equity would only have to

Paying For Options

go up a little under 3% annually in its overall price to be profitable. The second property, naturally, would have to appreciate 10% annually just to be of equal value in 5 years as it was when the option was granted.

Lets review the numbers:

Starting with an $80,000 value and using the final option price under our two methods, what is the the true annual rate of appreciation required?

$128,840.80 for 5 years = 10% annual rate of increase

$92,210.20 in 5 years = 2.9% annual rate of increase

Thus, in the first case, the property must increase at 10% or more to be a bargain to you, whereas the second place it only needs to go up 2.9% annually.

The Best Way

Best of all is a fixed price for the equity.

First you need not worry about appreciation to overcome the rate of price increase. But there is more. In our example above, we assumed the loan balance was $60,000 on day one and $60,000 at the end of year five.

This would only be true if the loan in the example were an interest only loan. If the loan was instead a 30—year, 13% new loan, there would be a principal paydown of $1,151.04 over 60 months and an equal amount of additional profit.

	Day One	Last (60th) month
option price	$20,000	$20,000
plus loans	$60,000	$58,849
	$80,000	$78,849

Note:
An option for equity gives the advantage of loan paydown, no matter if the option price for equity increases or is fixed.

Mind you, $1,151 isn't enough to make you rich. But our example is on one house—you could be optioning ten houses, or ten four-plexes. Also, we assumed a new 30- year loan. If the loan had been in existence longer, (which is more likely), it would have even a greater paydown over the 60-month term.

From another perspective, if the value was $80,000 at the end of 5 years, you'd be able to buy at a small discount. Even more important, since we assume your property will out perform the market average, you do not need to keep pace with some rate of market inflation, just to keep even.

If the equity buyout price goes from $20,000 to $32,000 or just remains at $20,000, in either case, the paydown on the loan benefits YOU.

Chapter Four

I remember an option I negotiated that had these two features canceling each other. The seller wanted a price that increased but hadn't argued about an option for the equity.

I went home and figured how much the loan decreased each year. It averaged about $2,000 annually per house. The average equity was $40,000 so I let him win by agreeing to a 5% annual increase, not compounded. We wrote the option price as follows:

> Year 1 ....$40,000 for the equity
>
> Year 2 ....$42,000
>
> Year 3 ....$44,000
>
> Year 4 ....$46,000
>
> Year 5 ....$48,000

Since the loan paid down about $8,000 per house over the 60 months, I really ended up with a fixed price for the whole property, (type 2) option, which wasn't bad at all!

The only way to improve on all this would be to have a fixed price for the equity, with a fast loan paydown and a lease with all the lease payments applying to purchase price—but that sounds too greedy.

Chapter Four

Part Two

Fast Cash Techniques

Chapter Five

Fix-Up And Sell

There is a great deal of money to be made in buying properties at a depressed price, due to "fixable" problems, solving those problems, then selling the property at full retail. In fact, some long term investors who are good at repairs and have a sharp eye for minor flaws in a property that can be corrected, will buy such a property to fix and hold. This way they get the benefit of a smaller purchase price and do not have to pay taxes on the gain that they achieve as they would if they were to sell.

There are a great many risks in the fix-up and sell format. One of the most obvious is the large amount of capital and the liability for debt. We can help reduce this risk with the use of an option. But before we cover that subject, let's look at some of the other risks that are a part of the total picture. (I wouldn't what you to learn the solution for the major problem and be undermined by several little problems!)

Avoiding A Mistake

1. Probably the biggest risk is that of doing the wrong repairs. This can happen primarily in two ways.

    You do the things that no one will pay extra money for.

    You do things that no one will pay extra money for in this neighborhood, this price of house or this particular style of house.

    The first type of "wrong repairs" mistake is the easiest to see. No one will pay you $15,000 more for an upper bracket home in Michigan if you buy the home and put in a $15,000 pool. However, it is almost impossible to go wrong making the kitchen modern.

    In the second case, even a kitchen could be a mistake. I once worked on a rehab project. This had been a working class project that, due to the depressed economic conditions in this "oil belt" community, had kept full by renting to low income immigrants. The rehab work was needed because the apartments had practically been abandoned by the former owners. The current tenants were good tenants in the units that were rentable. But it would have been a mistake to put back a dishwasher into those units that were being rehabbed to accommodate more of the same kind of tenants.

As the manager pointed out, people were more concerned with safe, clean accommodations than with having every modern convenience.

"Make them clean and fix the plumbing," she said. And in this location, at this point in time, she was correct. Whenever an owner is highly motivated he or she may be receptive to a price adjustment--it never hurts to ask.

2. Doing the repairs wrong.

I know this sounds a little basic. But it is true. In fact, I have read national figures that say that most "handy" owners are not all that handy at all. More than half of them mess-up on self improvement projects.

The risk here is that you will pay three times. You'll pay to do it wrong, pay to take it out, then pay to put it in correctly the last time.

The improvements that pay best are generally done in the bathrooms and kitchens. Those areas are both high use areas and areas in which styles and technical improvements (or the lack of them) are most noticeable.

With the assumption that you know what to spend your money on, let's look at another area of risk in fix-up purchases and how you can reduce that risk.

No Double Down Payments

The first step in acquiring a fixer, after you locate it, is to negotiate for the purchase. I have used a technique I call "no double down payments.

I point out to the seller that although I want very much to buy his house, I do not want to pay a double down payment. Most sellers will be quick to point out that they will be happy with just ONE down payment as they have outlined.

I say "No, you don't understand. You want a $20,000 down payment, which is normal for this priced property in this part of town. But your place will need about $20,000 to bring it up to perfect market shape. To me, that is a double down payment. For the $40,000 I will spend to buy from you, I could buy TWO properties that are not in as much need of repairs as yours."

I use this opening argument to try for a no down payment deal. Sometimes it works.

If the seller says that he could not sleep without a down payment, I reframe his comments like this: "You mean that it seems prudent to not do the deal unless I have something at risk? I've heard smart business people say the same. You are worried that if I do not have something to lose, I won't take good care of the property, right?"

Most sellers readily agree. Then I explain to him how I will have the $20,000 at risk, *the 20 I use to fix the property.* This, I point out, will be coming out of my pocket and therefore assures him that I will be financially committed to the property. Then it is time to try again for a nothing down purchase.

If this fails, I tell him I will put up the fix up money as a deposit. Rather than give him $20,000, I will put $20,000 in a title company account. This money will be used to do the repairs that need to be done. In fact, I will be more than happy to list the work that is to be done and supply bids to affirm the price for each task. I will only draw the money out as it is used to pay for the completed improvements.

If I fail to do the work, the $20,000 will be released to him as additional collateral for the money I still owe him, due to the note that he has carried back as part of the sale. If I complete the work, and I do not pay him on the note and he forecloses, all the problems in the property will have been corrected. How can he lose?

An Option Might Be The Better Way

There is still a risk to be dealt with ... and a second problem. The risk is the fact that your fix up efforts might not give you a profit. Let's assume you not only know what you are doing, you are careful at picking and pricing projects. Still, mistakes can be made.

Wouldn't it be better to use the fix up work you do as an OPTION to buy the property? Write the list of repairs you are going to put up as your option consideration. Have the sellers put a signed deed into escrow when you put in the money to do the work. When the work is done, you complete the closing.

You have several advantages. First you may avoid another problem. One of the problems of fixer properties is that you have to make payments on the property while you are doing the work. This increases your cash commitment and therefore it increases your risk.

Next, if you do run into a "nightmare," be that a major hidden structural problem or, a problem with a building inspector, you will be able to choose whether you want to toss in the towel and walk away from your repair money or close. I have known of situations where the problems were nothing compared to the loss from selling the property.

How To Protect Yourself

There are two primary protections that you must be aware of if you are to succeed with what I call "quick turn deals." In fact these two concepts can help you with all option deals and most all of your real estate deals in general.

Chapter Five

Problem number one... there is never enough time. I guess it's a combination of Parkinson's Law and Murphy's Law.

Parkinson said that the more time you have to do something, the more time it will take. If your option runs out in 60 days, it will take 60 days to get the property sold to another investor. You will not be done in 59 or 60 days... it will take all 60.

Everyone knows that Murphy guaranteed us more problems than we imagine. True to Murphy's law, something will go wrong on day 58 or 59 and that something will take 10 days to fix.

Solution: Have A Right To Extend

This is going to be especially important if you also need to fix or repair the property during your option or escrow period.

A right to extend might read like this:

> *"In the event buyer is unable to exercise option (or you could say to close" if you were using a contract format) in a timely manner, that being on or before _____ then buyer may obtain an extension with the payment of an additional $ _____ . This sum will act as consideration for a _____ day extension of the expiration date. (With a contract you'd say the "closing date.")*

Should buyer close during this extension, then the additional money paid will also apply to reduce the balance due (thus leaving a new balance due at time of closing of $ _____). If buyer fails to close then the additional money will be the property of the seller and forfeited by the buyer.

You may not have to pay for the right to extend, you may just get it as a part of the originally negotiated option. But if the additional money APPLIES to purchase, how are you hurt? If you got down to the last minute and the deal was falling apart, you would just forgo the whole deal. If you only needed a few days to wrap up a profit, you now have a way. NOTE: As an extra level of protection you may want to provide valuable consideration for any option extension. Remember this consideration may not be in the form of cash--whatever has value to both parties (services, upgrades, etc.) will suffice.

Whatever you do, get the right to extend when you do the initial deal. If you wait to ask for it the day you should close, you may be disappointed or it may cost you a great deal of money, money that does not apply to anything but getting an extension.

Fix-Up And Sell

The second big problem with "fixer" deals is that the seller might want to back out or even try to sell to another buyer. Most sellers don't have your imagination. If they did, they would not be selling to you at the price you are paying. When they see what wonders you have been able to accomplish with their property, they will realize just how cheaply they sold and they may not be as anxious to close as they were before.

If the worst situation occurs, they could sell the property out from under you and all you would have would be an expensive lawsuit on your hands.

Solution: Always Have Something Recordable

We have discussed the "Notice of Option" and its uses before. It is not only a good idea if you are improving a property you do not own, it is a must.

If you have a notice of option filed, then the property owner will have a very hard time changing his mind. If he tried to sell, no title company would give the new owners a title policy.

If the owner just decided not to sell to you at this time, he would have a cloud on the title that would stay forever. He would never be able to sell or borrow against that property again without coming to you.

Chapter Five

Chapter Five

Chapter Six

Options Are Like Listings Marketing Bargains

Options can either take the place of a listing or act as a listing. To take the place of a listing an option can be used by a real estate broker to control property when it is impossible to get a listing for one of several reasons. Secondly, an option can be used like a listing by people who do not have a real estate license. It is possible to use an option to get some of the same benefits you would be able to have if you had a listing on the property.

Out-Of-State Listings And Clients

When real estate brokers deal with properties and clients who do not live in the same state in which the real estate licensee has his license, there is a potential for a license law violation. In the simplest case, if a real estate licensee has a client who lives in the same state, but owns property in another state, the licensee can take a listing on the property. However, the licensee had best not do any marketing of that property outside the state. More specifically, state laws are usually violated when the agent brings potential buyers or potential financiers into that state to look at the property, a state where he is not licensed to sell property. He can, however, go into the state to look at the property himself and/or talk to local brokers, and leave without doing any marketing or agency activities.

A licensee who has a listing on an out-of-state property could go visit real estate brokers in that state and ask them if they would be interested in co-oping with him. There's no problem with this in that the real estate licensee from the state away from the property can work as a cooperating broker with a locally licensed person.

This, of course, is the cornerstone of the real estate marketing or real estate exchange meetings held around the country. So many investors are very upset when they hear that the real estate brokers do not allow unlicensed people to enter their meetings. They think they're trying to be exclusive or snobbish by not allowing non-agents to go to a marketing meeting. If a broker from California, who is not licensed in Texas, presents a property at a marketing meeting held in Texas, that California broker (who obtained the listing from a California resident) is in no trouble whatsoever *as long as all* the people at the real estate marketing session, *have a Texas real estate license*. HOWEVER, if an investor (or any non-licensed person) happens to be at that meeting, then the parties to the meeting all take a chance in being involved in a Department of Real Estate investigation. The out-of-state Broker/Agent who makes the presentation where a non-licensee is present, has probably violated the state's license laws.

Sometimes brokers joke that it doesn't bother them because how can they take away a license that they don't have? Well, in the state of Texas they can fine you, I believe, up to a $1,500 and can put you in the pokey for up to six months. Yes, there's a jail term available to out-of-state brokers who do business in the state of Texas without a Texas license or do business without co-oping through a licensed Texas broker. This law was passed because of all the abuses that occurred prior to the law's passage.

Another way for an out-of-state broker to deal on a property outside of the state in which the broker is licensed, is for that broker to get an option on the property.

EXAMPLE: Broker Herb lives in Ventura, California and he has been approached by a friend who owns property in Oregon. This friend says to Herb, "I hear you're a fantastic real estate exchange broker. I'd be willing to sell for cash or, preferably, trade for mini-warehouses anywhere in the United States. Would you be interested in taking a listing?"

The broker from Ventura sees the potential for violating license law. If he wants to advertise broadly that he has a property for exchange for mini-warehouses anywhere in the United States, he may end up doing "agency" business with non-licensees in a state in which he too doesn't have a license.

But, if the Ventura broker obtained an OPTION TO PURCHASE the property and that option agreement said that the owner of the property will sell the property for so many dollars cash, or will be open to acceptable properties in exchange for his property, then the licensee from Ventura has the ability to market the Oregon property anywhere in the United States.

You see, if you have an option to buy a piece of property, you're dealing as a principal. You are not acting as a real estate agent. You're offering to exchange your right to acquire the property for another property.

Chapter Six

If a cash buyer is found, you will simply take the difference from *your* sale price and your option price. If your option price is $500,000 and you "sell" at $540,000, you get $40,000 profit. The house owner can either take the $500,000 cash or use the cash through an escrow to buy a property to complete a "1031" tax-deferred exchange.

If you were offered a property in exchange and the original property owner would accept it, either the property owner or the property trader would have to add cash for you to profit.

NON-EXCHANGE EXAMPLE: A broker from Maine is an expert in seaside resorts. He sells a seaside resort in Maine for a client named Tom. Tom also has a resort in Florida and wants the broker to sell that for him too. Now, our broker travels to Florida frequently and is fairly familiar with the market down there. He also has built a very good relationship with the client and would like to continue that relationship by working on the Florida property. The Maine broker could take a listing on the property. However, a method that will allow the Maine broker far more latitude would be to take an option to purchase the property.

If the client wanted $2 million for the property and the commission for this type of transaction would normally be $75,000, and the broker felt that the pricing was right on the money and that the property was worth about $2.2 to $1.9 million, then the broker might tell the client that he'd take an option to buy the property for $1,925,000.

If the property is sold for $1,950,000, the broker makes $25,000. If the property brings $2.2 million, then his profit is much higher.

There is a risk in this sort of transaction. If you're dealing with an unsophisticated seller who really doesn't know what his property is worth, a broker could take advantage of that seller. The broker could get a low-priced option, knowing that the property was worth far more. Thus, the broker could earn far more than a normal listing commission if he priced the property low and it could have sold quite easily for more money.

The warning here to real estate brokers is to make sure that you get a reasonable price for the property, but not a "killer deal." It might come back to haunt you. If you buy the property for hundreds of thousands of dollars less than you sell it for, it's possible that the seller could go to court claiming that you played on his lack of knowledge about the true value of the property putting him at an unfair disadvantage. You got the listing so as to profit from his ignorance.

Years ago, states used to have something called "net listings." A net listing is when the seller was insistent that he wanted to net "X" number of dollars from his property. He didn't care how much you made (or in most cases, whether or not you made anything). He just wanted to make sure he netted what he wanted to net. The solution then was to sign a net listing. Because of the kinds of abuses that are available to someone using a net listing, (as we just described here with an option), net listings are illegal in most states.

Options When Listings Are Unobtainable

I witnessed a situation where an option was used by a real estate broker when a listing seemed nearly impossible to obtain. There were several owners to a piece of property. No one could get all the owners to agree to list at the same price and at the same time with the same real estate broker. This enterprising broker approached each of the owners of the property separately and obtained an option to buy that investor's share of the property separately and independently from all the others. Once he had obtained an option from each, he knew what his total price was. The options allowed him to market a property that was ripe for being sold for development when a listing seemed unobtainable.

Some real estate brokers have a hard time approaching a seller with the idea of a listing because the seller doesn't want to "mess" with selling the property. The example that comes to mind was a very wealthy man who owned many tracts of development ground. He really wasn't seeking a sale when this particular real estate broker approached him. He explained to the broker that he didn't need any money and he especially didn't have the time to review offers, counter-offers, sit in on negotiations, or put up with any of the usual hassles that are involved in the sale of real estate.

This innovative real estate broker asked the property owner if he could pay him a sum of money for an option to buy the property at a figure this sophisticated investor would gladly net with no hassle. He pointed out to the investor that he would either show up with a check for the full amount in hand or he wouldn't ever call him again.

An option is rather straightforward. If the option is for "X" number of dollars, all cash, you either come in with the cash or you don't. Once the potential for hassle was eliminated, the investor decided that he would give the broker a period of time to see if he could bring in an all-cash buyer.

Brokerage Without A Real Estate License

Investors can use options where listings cannot be obtained. For one reason or another, many investors do not want to obtain a real estate license. There are several valid reasons. One investor I talked to said that he was going to spend a year working on several real estate transactions while working an evening shift job. He wanted to earn enough money to put a down payment on a house for he and his wife, but did not want to make a career out of real estate. Many investors do not want to spend the time and effort necessary to get a real estate license. A real estate license only prepares you to represent other people and to help other people gain the benefits of professional sales assistance. These investors aren't interested in being an agent for another person. They're interested in dealing in real estate for their own personal profit.

Chapter Six

Sadly, some investors would like to act like a real estate broker, but not have to be subject to the scrutiny of the state. Hopefully, we don't have any readers that fall into the last category.

Looking at the second category, I've known many investors who would love to buy and sell out of their own portfolio, except that they don't have a portfolio. To get started, they get an option to buy one or more pieces of property. They'll try to negotiate an option at very favorable terms. They realize that if they have favorable price and terms on the property under option, they can sell that property for a slight profit and start building a nest egg to buy something for themselves.

These investors want short-term profits. Some want to buy bargain and keep them for long-term profits but still don't have cash.

I teach an entire series on the concept that we call "Down Payment Partners." The idea is that you find somebody else to put up the money for an especially lucrative transaction. If you're good at finding bargains and don't have any cash, this is an excellent way to get started. The concept, which is covered elsewhere in the book, tells you how to put your skills at finding bargain properties and solving property problems together with the money of people who don't have the time to mess with such transactions. One of the first steps in putting one of these deals together might very well be the obtaining of an option.

EXAMPLE: Let's say that you find a warehouse building that is easily worth $550,000. Because it is half empty, it's for sale at $400,000. You know of a friend of yours who's looking for warehouse space. You talk to him about leasing the warehouse and he says that it sounds perfect. He goes by and inspects it and is enthused with the idea. To keep him from exposing your position, you tell him you are negotiating to buy the building and you do not want the tenants or the property manager to hear about it too early — so he should just look and not talk.

After you have affirmed his interest and gotten his tentative agreement to lease, you approach the owner. Rather than just sign a real estate purchase contract, you obtain an option. In this option, you have the right to extend the option with the payment of additional cash. This additional option money will apply to purchase.

You can often get more time with an option than you can with a contract wherein you ask for a delayed close. A contract says you will buy and the general situation is that you use if for just that — so why delay? An option generally says you are going to buy, but you are unwilling to commit definitely right now. It is implied that you need some more time, for whatever reason and you are willing to put up some money to get into this position. The right to extend the time of closing is common in options. It is looked on with suspicion in purchase contracts.

Chapter Six

There is one more advantage to using the option in this situation rather than a contract. Not only is it legally a stronger claim on the equity, it is common to record an option, or as I suggest, a notice of option. If you get an option, with a right to extend, and get something recorded, you have done about as much as you can to make sure you will not lose the deal.

Now you have the right to buy the building for $400,000 and the tenant that will make it worth $550,000. (I'll assume you get something going with the tenant concerning the lease. It might even be possible to get the owner to sign the lease with the tenant before you fund the option. However, it would be safer to just get your purchase lined up quickly so you could close and lease the empty half the next day.)

You could go to investors and sell them the building for $550,000. I've done such deals before. But the more profit you try to make, the harder it will be to pull off this sort of deal. This is called "double escrowing." That is, you sign to pay up but you line up a new buyer that closes the same day you do, thus providing the money for the seller and leaving you with the profit.

I'm not saying this cannot be done. But two facts usually come into play. You will be presenting this package to a sophisticated buyer. Such people are very good at negotiating—and maybe a little better at it than you.

Furthermore, I have found that such buyers are good at finding out about the history of a property. If the potential buyer finds out that you have an option to buy at $400,000, it is very doubtful that he will pay you $550,000 without a fight. If he senses that you do not have the ability to do the deal without him, he will double his efforts to buy from you at $401,000 to $405,000, (whatever little amount of profit he thinks he can get you to take).

If, however, you can create the illusion that you can do the deal alone and move fast enough that the entire financial community does not know your business, this is one of the most profitable and exciting ways of making money in real estate.

Chapter Seven

Special Option Structure

Getting Paid Not To Buy: An Option To Cancel The Deal

Here is another interesting technique.

EXAMPLE: A man involved in an exchange wanted to give property that was worth several thousand dollars as a down payment and he was anxious for the other party to accept his terms. He said "Okay," but he "may" have a cash buyer in the wings.

This perplexed our man, who wanted to get something in writing now, without waiting for the seller to see if the cash offer was going to materialize.

So he said, "I'll tell you what, we'll go ahead and sign the deal and if you have a cash buyer for this very, very large amount that you think you might be able to get, then you can back out of our contract. *I'll give you an option to cancel the contract.*

If and when you want, you can give me $2,000 and get out of the contract with me. But, if you don't find the cash buyer, I'm signed and committed. Think of it as an insurance policy. You get the trade if and only if you can't get the cash."

This exchange formula intrigued me. And it came to mind later on. I had written and received acceptance on a contract to buy a small office building. My offer was at the asking price, which I considered too low. It was the first offer the seller received.

The day after it was put in escrow, the flier the broker had sent to MLS, (Multiple Listing Service), reached the hands of the investing public. Dozens of inquiries and several signed offers came in.

It didn't take the seller long to figure out that he had sold too cheap! You guessed it. He didn't want to close. The law was on my side, however. I could sue for specific performance. But the law, (and lawyers), are expensive and suits are no fun.

So, I remembered the exchanger's story. I told the seller, pay me $7,000 and you can cancel this deal. He had his agent bring over a check for $5,000 and I accepted it.

This seemed great. I got paid for NOT BUYING! (I avoided a potential fight and perhaps having to sue to force closing the deal.) The more I thought about it, the more the idea pleased me. "How could I do that again?" I wondered. And then I hit on an idea.

Many an investor would like to make low priced offers, but they know the odds of acceptance is so slight that it isn't worth the effort. Most sellers — even those between a rock and a hard spot — will hold out forever or until it is too late.

EXAMPLE: The seller wants $120,000 for his house, even though he is three payments late on the $75,000 loan on the property - and he refuses to consider your $77,000 offer.

SOLUTION: Give him the right to cancel the contract. Tell the seller, "We'll set up the closing now, but won't record anything for sixty days. If you get a firm contract for $80,000 or more, just give me $2,500 plus my earnest money back and we cancel the deal."

You might point out, "when worst comes to worst, usually there aren't any there. If all else fails, it is sold."

If somebody tells you they want to see if they can get a better deal - isn't that a beautiful way of overcoming an objection?

Read This Section Twice. It's A Real Money Maker! The Rolling Option

A rolling option is a psychological technique.

EXAMPLE: A fellow owns five houses and you want an option to buy all five. How much does he want? $50,000 and that's too much.

SOLUTION: Ask how much an option to buy ONE house would be. If the seller says $10,000, then you want a rolling option. You'll pay $10,000 for the right to buy the first house. If you fund or exercise the option within six months then you have the right to buy the second house, and so on.

If the owner agrees, that's fine. You write up a notice of option, put all five legal descriptions in there and then you file it.

Now, what have you done? You've acquired what you want with a PSYCHOLOGICAL technique. You'll pay less for a smaller option, but if you perform on that one you roll to the next, roll to the next, roll to the next.

Chapter Seven

If You Buy This →

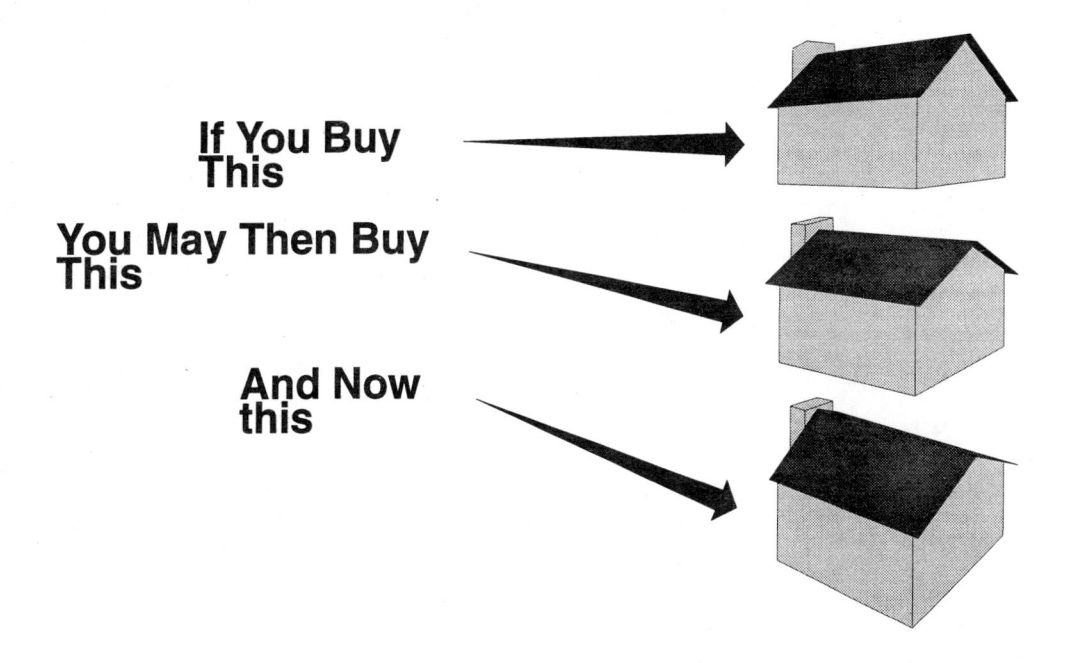

You May Then Buy This →

And Now this →

The idea of the rolling option is to negotiate an option on one of many properties one seller has for sale. This way the option price seems like it should be cheaper, but the roll over provision really lets you tie up all the properties. This is especially good for big pieces of land - when a builder buys lots as he builds.

First Right Of Refusal And Options

Here is another concept that I find to be fascinating. That is an option combined with a first right of refusal. Here's how it works.

EXAMPLE: You own a piece of property that's worth about $80,000. I have the right to buy it for $200,000. The option is good for 10 years. Five years from now the property is worth $160,000. My option is $200,000 so I still don't have any value in my option do I? But there is another five years to run and the price is moving up very nicely, thank you. It will be worth a good $320,000 at that rate, straight line, by the end of the option period.

You come to me and you say, "Barney, you have had this option for about five years. I thought I ought to tell you I'm going to sell the property to somebody else."

I had the option to buy his property for $200,000. (It's worth $160,000.) He can sell to somebody else; he just sells it subject to my option. *Whoever buys it has to remember that I have the right to buy it for the $200,000. They get a recorded notice of it.*

And, yes, he'll probably have to sell at a little bit of a discount. Because whoever buys it knows that the most they are ever going to get out of that property over the remaining five years is $200,000. Maybe he'll only get $140,000 when he sells it. *But if I have an option coupled with the first right of refusal, then I have the chance to pick up the bargain earlier if somebody wants to sell the property at below the option exercise price.*

If he wanted to sell the property that is worth $160,000, (which is far and away from my exercise price), to YOU for $140,000 I would tell him I'd buy it at $140,000. (Remember, I have the first right of refusal.) HOWEVER, I could turn around and ask if YOU would buy it at $160,000 if I canceled my option? You'd probably say yes.

I buy the property at $140,000 and sell it to you for $160,000. I get $20,000 for the cancellation of my option, which is probably very shortsighted in this particular example.

But you can see how it works. An option combined with the first right of refusal gives you the chance to pick up a bargain, if it is in the making, prior to the exercise time.

Chapter Eight

Option Solutions To Foreclosures

Options & Federal Tax Liens

In every case that I've been able to check out, if the IRS puts a tax lien on a property, and if the optionee can prove that the optioner, (who is also the person who owes the taxes), gave him a valid lease option or a valid option sometime in the past, the IRS will recognize that option as a prior claim.

This means that if you buy an option to purchase the property for $50,000, and the property goes up to $75,000 in value, the IRS lien goes on after your $50,000 option price. If the existing loans against the property are $35,000, you can write the IRS a check out for $15,000 and you own the property subject to $35,000 in liens.

If you don't have *something recorded*, they will probably never call you. If you can prove conclusively that you have a *valid option*, not one concocted to get around an IRS lien, then you have a good chance of being able to protect your interest.

BY REPORTING THE "NOTICE OF AGREEMENT CONCERNING A LEASE"—WITH A SILENT OPTION, (unrecorded and undisclosed), you probably can avoid conflict on the "due--on--sale" issue and protect your interest from other creditors all at the same time.

A due-on-sale clause, sometimes referred to as an alienation clause, provides the lender the right to call all sums owing if the borrower conveys title of the property to another party by sale, trade or agreement of sale prior to paying off the loan. Most all these clauses are very broadly drawn to include any sort of transfer except a lease of less than three years.

Other creative strategies will work, but I'm sure you can find many ways to get yourself into trouble without additional suggestions! Remember, that while "violating" the "due--on--sale" may not be a criminal offense in most situations, it should not be done without legal advice. Federally insured lenders have special regulations that my take precedence. Those with real estate licenses will want to obtain a professional legal opinion concerning their situation and obligations. Other than that, all "due-on-sale" avoidance strategies may work, if the Savings and Loan doesn't check.

Redemptive Rights Are Like Options

Several states have the system of redemptive rights. If a property owner lets his property go into foreclosure, he has the right to redeem the property by paying off the back due balance, (and usually some interest).

That right is really an option for his property, and that redemptive right can be assigned to others. It is just like buying an option on a piece of property. If somebody has the redemptive right to buy the property in the next six months, it's just like an option to buy the property and you can buy that redemptive right from him.

In many states, the redemptive period runs from the day of the foreclosure to the day of (or just before) the sale.

In Kansas, you get six months to "bail out" your home if you lose it to foreclosure. Being a homestead state this period is after the sale as well as before.

EXAMPLE: We found a house that was "bid in" by the lender two days earlier. (The lender bought the house at the sale, deciding the lower bids were not acceptable.) We rented the house from the now foreclosed upon owners for six months at $200 per month, all prepaid—and in addition received the option to buy the redemptive rights for $100 more, to be paid if we later wanted to own the house.

We leased the house *the same day* for $600 per month and got a $600 security deposit! The total cost--$1,200 and total income--$3,600. Total out--of--pocket --$0. Not bad for not owning the house!

We did several of these and always tried to bargain with the lender during the six month redemptive right period. But I guess we never offered enough money or maybe the lenders were a touch mad at us! But that doesn't mean you couldn't get a good buy as well as the cash flow!

Discounted Sale - Option To Buy Back

This is one of my favorite techniques. For many years, I used this financial maneuver to close on high risk deals.

Let's review a typical deal, that is based on one of mine.

A developer approached me looking for cash. He had developed a subdivision in the Ozarks in violation of the Federal Land Sales Act. That cost him more money than he had. He saved his subdivision but was about to go under.

Option Solutions To Foreclosures

His only meaningful unencumbered asset was a $150,000 first mortgage secured by forty acres of land that had subdivision potential. Other areas near there had been broken up into large lot subdivisions.

This developer wanted me to loan him $100,000 secured by the note. He wanted the money for one year.

Well, I'm not a bank and I do not make loans very often. Besides, if I made the loan and he did not pay it, I would have to sue on the note. If I won that suit, I'd end up with the first mortgage. If the first mortgage did not pay, I would have to foreclose on the first. If I got the land, I'd have to sell it to get my cash. And "to be developed" land is very hard to sell. This did not sound like the way to have fun.

The land was worth at least $240,000. That made me feel a little better about the note. The note was properly drawn and secured as a first with an interest rate of 15%. All this was good news.

I offered to buy the note for $75,000. The developer had a fit. He said he was desperate but not that desperate.

Time would soon tell. If no one else stepped forward soon, my first offer would have been his only hope. But I assumed he would say "no" and I had a second offer in mind.

"Do you think things will be better for you?" I asked. "Will you be out of the woods in six months or a year?"

He assured me that it would only take six months, but if everything went wrong, his situation would surely be improved in a year.

Then I offered to buy the note for $75,000 and give him the option to buy it back in one year for 10% more. That seemed to appeal to him. I told him to think of it as a pawn shop loan. If fact I refer to this technique as the "Zick Pawn Shop Loan."

The steps are quite simple. I pay $75,000 for the note and he will assign it to me. At the same time I will give him a sheet of paper that says he has the option to repurchase the note for $75,000 plus 10% or $7,500, for a total of $82,500.

What about my return? The note is paying 15%. I keep the interest-only payments during the term of my holding the note. And remember, I bought it at half price. Thus I have 30% so far. And the buyback is for 10% more. In simple terms, I am making 35%. Not bad. And if he does not buy back, I make a little better return.

This technique allows you to have an asset fully assigned to you at a very, very low price. If the seller buys it back, you have a good return. But the safety factor, considering the collateral, is super.

Chapter Eight

I personally do not do this sort of transaction with the "public." It is not a substitute for a normal loan or a way to get around state usury laws. (In fact, some states will say that this sort of structure violates their usury laws.) It is a way to deal with high risk people, who are in such a mess that no one will extend them any additional credit.

In an upcoming text, "Aggressive Acquisition Techniques," I plan to give you a dozen variation of this technique. But this discussion should be enough to show you how an option figures into this situation.

Option To Buy Back To Revalue Asset

An option to buy back is also a way of revaluing an asset. Its basic structure is the same as the Pawn Shop Loan.

EXAMPLE: You think your land is worth $200,000, and I think it's worth $100,000. You say you have to sell it; you need to raise some cash. I say I'll buy it but I'll only pay $100,000. You say that you'll do that but you want an option to buy it back in a year at $110,000. That way if you are right — that it's worth more, you'll get a 10% return on your money. If you don't buy it back, then I got it for what I thought it was worth. **It helps revalue the price.**

I might say I want a little better deal than that. I'll buy it at $80,000 and give you the right to buy it at $110,000 or something like that.

The discounted sale option buy back has also been used to bring undesirable properties down to a bargain level. In this way they can be sold quickly, but if they are worth more later on, then you can still recoup your money.

This concept also works well in an exchange. Each property type has its basic level of desirability. Cash has more utility, in general, than a rented building and the building more than land.

EXAMPLE: A has a building, (which has income and depreciation), and B has the $200,000 in land. To induce A to take his land in a trade, B could value the land at $100,000, with an option to buy it back. A gives $100,000 worth of credit toward the building value. If B buys back, A gets cash. If he doesn't, A gets a $200,000 piece of land for $100,000, which might ease the pain of not getting cash!

Chapter Nine

How To Get Income Tax Breaks With Options

An Option Is Not Taxed Until Exercised

Let's talk about the tax consequences of the option.

This is very, very important. It is one of the key features of an option.

If I own a piece of property and you get an option from me and you pay me $10,000 for that option, **the money I receive is not taxed to me at all until the option is exercised, is vacated or expires.** (Exercised means you go ahead and buy the property. If you no longer want the option or if I pay you to give it up, it is "vacated." And the expiration date is just that.)

According to the IRS, an option is taxed according to the nature of the property on which it is placed. If you have an option on real estate you look at how real estate is taxed. So if I have an option that is a 13 or 14--month option, then it's a long term option. If I have an option that is a 5--month option, then it's a short term option and the taxes are based on long term (capital gain) or short term (ordinary income) tax rates. Check current laws to see how many months of holding are required to be classified "long term." Right now it is six months.

If I own a piece of property and you buy a 13--month option from me for me $10,000 and you don't exercise it and it expires, I have a $10,000 long-term capital gain. If I have a 5--month option and it expires, I have a short term capital gain, which is ordinary income. *Option money received is not taxed until the option is exercised or expired.*

One of the best ways to persuade a seller-optionor to agree to an option arrangement with you is this:

The tax benefits to the seller in 1938, in the Virginia Iron Coal and Coke Company v. Commission of Internal Revenue (99F. 2d919) the court decided that money received under a lease option contract that will be credited toward the option is to be considered "indeterminate income."

The question was this:

Should an owner claim monthly option money as rent, and therefore subject to the existing income tax rates, or should it be claimed as part of the down payment, and therefore subject to whatever tax rules are in effect at the time.

The taxpayer in this case did not claim the option money until the lease was breached, believing that until the lease was breached or the option exercised a taxable event had not taken place. The IRS challenged the taxpayer.

The Court ruled that an event must have occurred before the IRS can tax option money. If the optionee-buyer breaches the lease the optionor-owner would declare all sums previously received as option money, and pay whatever ordinary income tax was due. If the option were exercised, then, in the year of the sale, the money would be applied to the down payment.

What this means is this:

An owner is able to spend the option money and not pay taxes on it until either the option is exercised or the lease is broken.

For the seller this means then, that he or she could collect several thousand dollars as option money up front and collect so much per month as option money--and not have to pay taxes until much later.

If you exercise the option short term, it's just part of the down payment money. It's like a slow close. The option money is just like an escrow deposit — but it's held by the seller rather than an escrow company or attorney or broker.

If you exercise the option long term, it's still just like part of the earnest money deposit with the down payment money and I'd figure my taxes on the sale of the whole thing forgetting there ever was an option in the first place. Even though I might have gotten the option money 2-3 years before the time of sale, I just include it in the down payment consideration at time of sale.

If you give me $10,000 to buy an option and you let the option expire short term, you have an ordinary loss. You can write off against your earned income. If the option is held for whatever term the IRS calls "the long term holding period," which since early 1985 has been over six months, and you let it expire, then you have a long term capital loss.

If you exercise the option, the option money becomes down payment money and you forget about the length of time. It's as if you put a down payment up one year and much later you finish the closing. For tax purposes, that money is

Chapter Nine

How To Get Income Tax Breaks With Options

just added to your basis in the property. (Basis is what you "have it on your books for.")

Since 1988, the maximum Capital Gains Tax has been 28%, which is the same as the maximum income tax (not counting the 5% surcharge). However, the rate may change with a more favorable rate for capital gains in the future.

This is the reason I said I don't care if your option money applies or doesn't apply, because in either case, the option money just adds to your basis in the property when you exercise it.

I would not recommend for you to plan your entire investment scheme around this idea — because it might backfire on you. But, in one court situation, there was a man who bought five options. He paid a lot of money on the first and a dollar on the other options. The first option expired in eleven months and the next option expired after that, and so on.

He had different options, and every time an option expired, he wrote it off his income taxes. The price he was going to pay for the property went down each time he made option money payments. So he was receiving the same benefit as if he was writing his down payment money off over a period of time, (which you can't do!)

A judge upheld this as being valid, separate options. The IRS fought it. The IRS lost. That amazed me. I would never hang my hat on that case. You know how the IRS is. You just figure out what you want and they rule the other way around. I was surprised they were able to write it all off, but the idea was too novel not to mention it!

Profit By Selling Options - Don't Exercise Them

A student of mine once said, "Barney, if I had an option to buy a piece of property for $100,000 and the property grew to be worth $200,000, I'd never make the profit anyway because I'd never be able to get the $100,000 together to buy the property in the first place."

So, I said, "NO. NO. NO." You don't have to get the $100,000 to get the property. *You sell the option.* If the property is worth $200,000 and the option is at $100,000, then the value of the option is worth $100,000.

You find somebody to buy the property. You ask him to write his check out for $200,000 and give it to the escrow company. Then you go to the person that has the property on which you have the option. You say, "You are going to get your $100,000. Go down to the escrow company. Sign the deed. Put the deed in escrow."

As the seller, you will get $100,000 for the property and I will assign my option into escrow and sell it for $100,000. Thus, the buyer has paid $200,000.

If I held my option long enough, I get long term capital gains on the selling of the option.

Chapter Nine

I knew a man who was supposed to be wise and knowledgeable. He had a huge trailer park in Florida under option for five years and I was going to trade for it. I said, "You want me to trade for the option don't you?" He said, "No. We'll just close one day and I'll deed it to you the next. It doesn't make any difference."

Wrong. The guy had realized a million dollars in profit. (The tax man would probably drive out to your house to talk about that. He wouldn't even ask you to come down to the local office. Right?)

I tried to explain to him. He said his CPA said it didn't make any difference. I don't know what CPA stood for in this case, but it didn't stand for Certified Public Accountant. His CPA probably knew what was correct, most likely he just misunderstood him.

You do not fund on an option, (exercise the option and acquire title to the property), and turn around and sell. Why? Because the IRS would ask how long your holding period was.

Your original holding period on the option was perhaps one year. Then you bought the property by exercising the option. Now you hold the property, not the option. How long did you own that? 3-1/2 seconds. That's short term. And, you have a million dollars worth of taxes due on a short term gain.

This also holds true for my "partnerships." When I do my option partnership with you, you give me $50,000 to buy a property in your name. I have the option to buy half interest in that property for $25,000.

If the property goes up in value, and we sell, I sell my option, my claim to a half interest in the property into escrow. I get the profit, less the $25,000 that goes to you. If I've held that for over a year, I get long term capital gains on my option.

If the tax law concerning Capital Gains is changed, as is being proposed, the difference between long and short term tax treatment will be important again.

Option To Option

EXAMPLE: I have just signed an option to purchase a great investment house. It had been presented at a local marketing session. A fellow broker/investor discovered I had closed the deal and was upset. She had planned to make an offer but she hadn't gotten around to it.

My option cost me $5,000 to buy the house for $60,000 anytime in the next 24 months, with the option money applying. The first loan was $47,500.

My business acquaintance said she had been prepared to offer $63,000 for the house. (I did have a good buy! I felt the house was worth $70,000.)

Always open to opportunities for profit, (with more good deals than money), I offered her my option for $8,000. She agreed.

Chapter Nine

How To Get Income Tax Breaks With Options

If I were to take $8,000 cash, with a six-day holding period, I would have realized $3,000 of ordinary income. Back then, I was more of a speculator and had already turned too many non-tax effect deals that year already. If I could delay the sale to next year, (two months), at least taxes wouldn't be due until April 15th of the *following* year! If I could get that gain taxed as capital gains, all the better. Here was our solution.

SOLUTION: The new option holder didn't want to exercise the option for *at least* a year anyway. And she only had $5,000 cash now, not $8,000. **So, we agreed that I give her an option to purchase my option.** She paid me $5,000 with $3,000 due to me at exercise or purchase of my option. Her right to buy my option lasted 13 months and could not be exercised for 12 months!

I got all my money out and just had to wait to see which way I profited.

Establishing A Basis In Your Option

When I set up a partnership, even though I'm buying the property at whatever it is worth today and my income is not going to be realized until way off in the future, I'll tell my bookkeeper to put me down for $2,000 profit on this new option.

The $2,000 will be taxed as ordinary earned income. Even though it has no value, I want to pay taxes on $2,000 worth of value in this option partnership. I do that to establish a basis in the property. My alternative is to wait 10 years and make a million dollars on my option partnership and have the IRS say that's all ordinary income. They would love to claim that the whole thing is basically a commission.

I'll say, no, that my commission is $2,000. I already paid taxes on that. Now that I paid taxes on it, I'm invested in the option. Everything over $2,000 is now long term capital gains.

Chapter Nine

Chapter Nine

Chapter Ten

Tax And Financial Planning

Options And Estate Freezing

Options can be an excellent method of "estate freezing."

EXAMPLE: You have a net worth of nearly $800,000 and no spouse. You have two children to whom you would like to leave the bulk of your estate. $600,000 of your net worth is in real estate equities. (We are going to assume that these are very conservative figures, your properties could be worth a lot more).

You're 58-years-old and plan to live a long life. However, you don't like the idea of Uncle Sam taking a large chunk out of your estate. You think your portfolio is extremely well positioned for future appreciation and since you are a professional and still earning a strong income, you are not worried about spending the cash flow kicked off by your properties. You've kept your portfolio in a "growth" position for quite some time. (That means, periodic refinancing when cash flow is high enough to service another loan. Many older investors convert their growth portfolio to a cash flow portfolio with the intent of using the cash for retirement. This doesn't relate to you.).

> **"All tax strategies work if you are not audited!"**
>
> *Danny Santucci*
>
> *Attorney at Law*
>
> *Newport Beach, CA*

One of the ways to keep control of your property without giving the management and directive powers away, while still freezing your estate, is to give your children option to purchase the property at today's value. If each of your children had the right to buy a one-half/undivided interest in your $600,000 net worth portfolio, with an option price of $600,000, then they would benefit from any future appreciation from today forward.

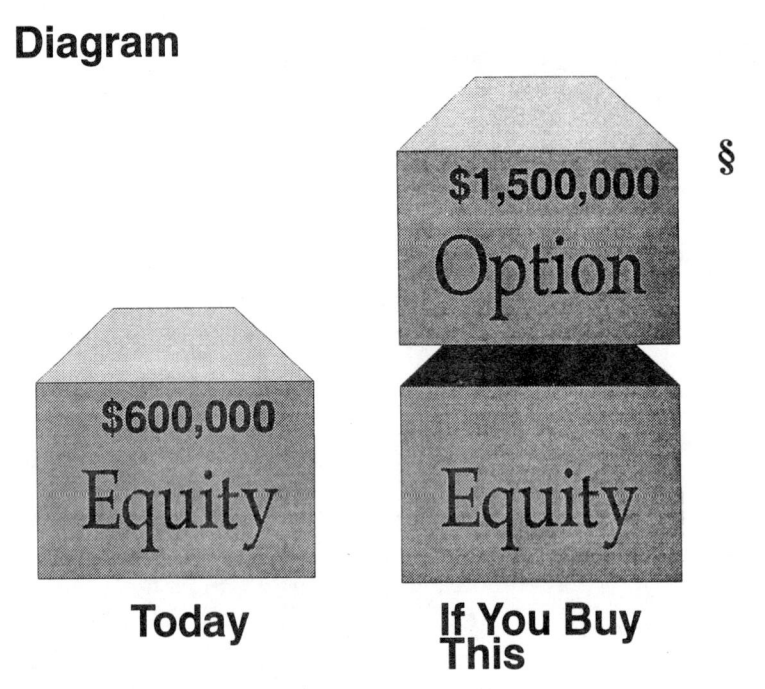

Diagram

$600,000 Equity — Today

$1,500,000 Option / Equity — If You Buy This §

§ Profit in option, not taxed to you!

You'd still have the ownership and the depreciation from the properties. You'd have total day-to-day operating control of these properties. The children would have the future appreciation.

After you're dead, the $600,000 in properties would be included in your estate and given to the children, but if they were then worth $1.5 million, the additional $900,000 would not be taxed in the estate. That value already belongs to your children by way of the option.

At one time I worked on an option with an individual who was concerned about liquidity of his estate. We combined an option with a life insurance policy. You could use that idea in this case. You could buy a life insurance policy and name a trustee for your children as the beneficiary. The policy could be used to pay any taxes that were due, pay all costs of administrating the estate, so that no real estate would have to be sold to cover costs.

Chapter Ten

Tax And Financial Planning

Options And The Financial World

There are dozens of combinations of life insurance and options that could work for you.

You should see a qualified estate tax lawyer, especially one who has knowledge of real estate, to help you work out these ideas.

How does the financial world view options? Well, they don't give you nearly as much credit as you'd like, but then again, options can be a tremendous boost to your financial statement.

Odds are, a bank will not be willing to loan you money against an option. Banks consider them intangible personal property and not real estate. Besides, it's hard to protect an option because it usually is in a secondary position. If there's already an existing first and second mortgage on the property, your option really is in third position and that would make their lien against your option in fourth position. That's just not what a conservative institution like a bank wants to see.

I *have* been able to borrow money against an option. I did so by showing the value of the option to a very savvy real estate investor. I then gave him a note secured by the option as a down payment on another piece of property. The option had a value of around $40,000. The note I gave him was only $10,000 and was a short term note. He figured that if he didn't get paid for my note, he would gladly take the option instead.

You can get the best use of options on your financial statement for "Show and Tell" purposes. They really look good.

EXAMPLE: How would a normal piece of property show up on your financial statement? On the asset side you'd show a rental house for $85,000. On the liability side you'd show $70,000 in loans. This would show your net worth at $15,000 if there were nothing else on your financial statement. Your assets would be long term assets and your net worth would not be a very "liquid-looking" net worth. If you had three such properties, you'd show $45,000 in net worth but $210,000 in liabilities.

STATEMENT A

Assets $255,000 *Liabilities* $210,000

3 SFH

Net Worth $ 45,000

Total Assets $255,000 $255,000

Chapter Ten

Contrast this with someone who holds options. You would show $15,000 option contract equity for each option. *That would give you an asset and something to add to net worth with absolutely nothing on the liability side.* In this example, you'd have $45,000 in "Option Contracts" and $45,000 net worth and NO liabilities.

While it is true that not all lenders will treat options as assets, enough of them will to make it worth your while to list them as such.

STATEMENT B

Assets $45,000 *Liabilities* --0--

Contract Equity

Net Worth $45,000

Total Assets $45,000 $45,000

Mix $100,000--$200,000 worth of options in with a normal financial statement of a real estate investor, and all of a sudden your assets - to - liabilities ratio starts looking better and better.

No. Lenders usually won't loan you money against options, but when they look at your overall financial picture, they are impressed when they see items on the asset's side that don't have liabilities.

Some investors carry options under the section called "Contracts Receivable." This might seem like stretching the truth, but there isn't a section on the normal bank's financial statement that calls for options, and Contracts Receivable is about as close as a description as any. Of course you should note somewhere on the financial statement that this "receivable" is an option.

Options And Bankruptcy

Options are in a peculiar situation when it comes to bankruptcy. If a person holds an option contract, odds are he'll end up owning that option after the bankruptcy — even if it has been shown on the financial statement and the entire world knows that he has it. Here's how it works.

All contracts in motion, which the courts call "Executory Contracts," need quick action. The bankruptcy law says that within 90 days of filing bankruptcy, the bankruptcy trustee has to execute (act on) these contracts or turn them back to the debtor.

If a bankruptcy trustee is looking at large dollar amounts of liabilities and no cash, his only concern is where to raise cash. He isn't about to write a check to fund an option.

A lease option also comes with the liability of continuing to make lease payments. The lease part of a lease option is a liability. An option to buy a

Tax And Financial Planning

one-half/undivided interest in a property must be one of the worst items to write a check for if you are the bankruptcy trustee. He or she would be buying into a partnership when most trustees would be trying to get cash out of all partnerships.

So, if you are in the unfortunate circumstance of filing for bankruptcy, don't make a big fuss over demanding your options back "because they're so valuable" or you might convince the bankruptcy trustee of their value. Just be patient. You probably will have them turned back over to you eventually anyway.

ON THE OTHER SIDE OF THE COIN, if somebody owes you money, you might want to show up for the bankruptcy hearing. I made offers on properties involved in bankruptcies and once sold a 254-unit apartment complex out of bankruptcy. I was trying to buy it myself but just couldn't qualify for the nothing down purchase I had arranged.

My buyer waltzed in and picked up 254 units for $25,000 down! Amazing as it may seem, literally no one shows up for bankruptcy hearings. The bankrupt person and his attorney are there and maybe one other person. If you're owed money in a bankruptcy, and the judge is about to toss the real estate investors options back to him, **you might ask for the options yourself, for payment of monies due you.** (I got a $50,000 fee. I'd rather have had the apartments.)

Of course, this would take a little bit of investigation on your part to find out what the real value of the options are, if any. If the person has made enough mistakes to end up in bankruptcy, he might not be the most savvy investor around. But then again, some bankruptcies occur from isolated events or non-reoccurring events, and it might have been one large problem that caused the bankruptcy of an otherwise sage investor.

Needless to say, it's an interesting thought to remember if you're ever caught on either side of the bankruptcy coin.

Chapter Ten

Chapter Ten

Part Three

Cash Flow Techniques

Chapter Eleven

Lease Options

What Are Lease Options

On the continuum of ownership, with no ownership (and no right to use) on one end and full ownership and use on the other, renting and then lease option are in the middle!

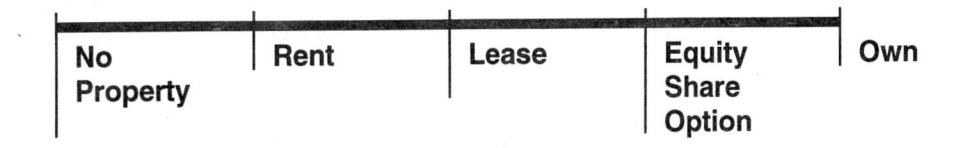

| No Property | Rent | Lease | Equity Share Option | Own |

Who knows why the first lease option came about? All parties have so many potential benefits and therefore motives to contract under a lease option. Let's assume a farmer, (serf), told his landlord (king) that he would rent farmland — but only if he could buy the land later. He didn't like the idea of turning pasture into cropland, only to have it go back to someone else. Or perhaps it was the king's way of giving the serf a reward in the form of a chance for ownership. Who knows! But it still goes on today.

In more recent history, no one cared much about lease option, until the early 1950s. Those who rented did so out of convenience or necessity. Those who bought, found a way, sooner or later.

After World War II, housing prices started to climb rapidly.

Housing Prices

It became apparent to many renters that by the time they saved the money to buy, prices had escalated just enough to force them to wait and save more. And this looked to be a never-ending cycle.

Landlords had few problems until the late 1960s. Rents had never kept pace with increasing prices, but the problem began to get worse. Prices rose substantially, especially in relation to rents, and in addition, a new rental homeowner had to put quite a bit more money down to make a house break even. Interest rates were on the rise too.

Chart Of Home Prices And Mortgage Interest Rates

Year	Starter Home Price	Effective Interest Rate
1975	$28,700	9.36
*	*	*
1978	$39,200	9.19
1979	$44,700	10.39
1980	$50,000	12.53 §
1981	$54,700	14.07
1982	$56,800	15.77
1983	$58,100	13.33
1984	$60,600	12.17
1985	$63,000	12.40
1986	$66,400	10.75
1987	$71,900	9.28
1988	$75,300	9.18
1989	$77,800	9.78

§ The National Average Mortgage Contract Interest Rates and Home Prices are for the first quarter of each year, which were taken from the First-Time Home buyer Affordability Index published by the National Association of Realtors.

This "double whammy" made it so that by the end of the '60s, principal, interest, taxes, insurance, maintenance, and management exceeded rent, in all but a few new purchases.

How do you induce the tenant to pay more? What tenant NEED could a landlord meet to induce higher than normal rental payments? *A one-year lease with a fixed price to buy became popular.* It solved the owner's cash flow problem and, for those tenants who hoped to own a home someday, it reduced their fear that prices would continue to grow beyond their reach.

The value given for value received varied greatly. In some cases, landlords who really wanted to sell couldn't find a buyer who was fully qualified. The "buyer"-or would-be-buyer - was only qualified as a tenant, despite his desire to own. Thus, the lease came with a reasonably priced option and perhaps all the rent applied to the purchase. Some of these agreements included a right to renew them.

At the other extreme, naive renters, who could never qualify for a loan, (even given one year to improve their lot), were silly enough to pay more rent to include the option to buy, just to relieve the anxiety about their dilemma as perpetual renters.

The option and lease expired in a year and the terms were "all cash at closing." Landlords accepting this sort of deal don't win in the long run. As the lease nears expiration and the tenant realizes he has no chance of ownership despite the fact that he has paid higher rent for the option, there is the temptation to "skip out" on the lease.

Today some tenants insist on an option with the lease - and they never buy. Reasons?

1. "If we really like it here, we will want to buy."

2. "If we put a lot of money into it we'll want to buy it."

3. "If it really goes up in value we want to have the option of buying."

4. "If the U.S. has another round of inflation, we will want to have an option to buy."

5. "If prices go up again this year like they did in this area last year, we will want to able to buy."

Whatever the stated reason, some don't want to face the reality that they are unable to buy or think they can fool their peer group by equating a lease-option with ownership.

We are a very mobile society and want (or are forced) to move frequently. Most of the early landlords, (who did lease options in the 60s), told me that NINE OUT OF TEN PEOPLE DID NOT BUY AT THE END OF THE LEASE. That is, not unless the lease option was so favorable to the tenant as to be a disguised sale. And the same is true today. **If the lease option is not really a creative alternative for a purchase, most tenants give up the option at the end of the lease and just move on.**

Chapter Eleven

Pro Tenant Or Owner—Who Wins?

The motivation and benefits for both the buyer and seller are so varied — either or both parties can get a super deal.

What would motivate someone to give you a lease option?

1. *They have a vacant rental(s) and don't have time to spend finding a tenant.* Running ads in the "lease option" column of your paper and the "for sale" column, (where you mention "rent to own"), gives you more exposure to more potential takers for your property.

    Besides, if you are tired of tenant turnover, you could give a long term lease option.

2. *They have been poor landlords and therefore have had more than their share of management problems.* Owners take better care of the property than straight renters. Usually, tenants that hope or expect to own someday will act more like owners than renters! Thus, management problems, such as repairs or even vandalism, should be less with a lease option occupant.

3. *The property is in poor shape and if they are going to keep it they must put cash into repairs.* Nothing makes an owner more nervous than undertaking major repairs and fix up (due to tenant neglect) - in order to attract a better quality tenant, and then rent again.

    It is not uncommon on the west coast, (or anywhere during periods of fast price increases), to require upfront option consideration of five percent of the selling price - at least $5,000 to $10,000. This could be used to finance needed repairs without the landlord coming out of pocket or borrowing the money.

4. *They just lost the property manager.* And now, rather than try to replace this manager, the lease option is an alternative.

5. *They are about to move.* They have been good property managers and they know what is required to stay on top of things. The idea of long distance management frightens them but they don't want to sell the property.

    The potential higher quality tenant in a lease option could allow them to continue ownership, (thus continue to receive the tax write-off) and delay or avoid a sale. This could be especially important if they have several rental houses in the same area. They wouldn't want to put all of the houses on the market at once and flood the market. This way their tax liability could be spread over several years.

6. *Vacancies are a frequent occurrence and they are tired of rental management.* This is a primary motivation. High tax bracket owners are forced to keep properties when the fun of landlording has long passed.

    With a lease option, they get to keep the tax benefits without the usual tenant problems.

Chapter Eleven

Lease Options

7. *The owners tried to sell.* Giving a tenant a lease option isn't as good as a sale, if you want to sell, but it is a lot better than leaving the house vacant.

What will absentee owners or passive investors get from giving you a lease option?

1. *Tax write-offs from depreciation, deduction of taxes, interest and insurance.*

2. *No management headaches.* (Especially with a motivated renter/buyer.)

3. *No maintenance, sometimes!*

4. *Usually enough cash to pay the existing loans.*

5. *Relief from many ownership responsibilities,* (i.e.: showing property when vacant, if you give a long term lease option.)

If you work it right, as an optionee tenant, you'll get:

1. *Control of an investment asset with little cash.* Let's face it, "standard business practice" says you put less money down on a lease option than you do when you buy. Ten percent down on a purchase is considered skimpy, whereas it would be a large option payment.

2. *Appreciation.* Properly structured, all or part of the increase in property value, due to an increase in demand or due to inflation, could be yours.

3. *Positive cash flow, potentially.* If your lease option property can be rented to another, (sandwich lease*), for a break-even today, you can be sure that subsequent rent increases will give you a positive cash flow!

*Sandwich lease discussed in next section.

Lease Option/ Sandwich Lease

With a sandwich lease the owner leases to me and I lease to somebody else, who is the user. I have a sandwich position. I'm sandwiched between the owner and the user.

Sandwich lease positions can be profitable from quite a few points of view.

One, if the owner wants a passive investment, and you're doing a sandwich lease, YOU deal with the user.

In some California houses that I have leased for passive investors, over a five year period of time there were six tenants! Others had the same tenant for 5 years! I've been able to keep vacancies down to just a few days and move tenants in, acting as a buffer for the passive owners. They didn't have to spend the time or money on vacancies.

Chapter Eleven

The Ultimate Example

You've seen the Johnny Carson Show. It's shot in Burbank but produced in Century City, California, a development of the Alcoa Aluminum Corporation. When that project started, it almost fizzled. It loped away from the gate. It was very, very expensive, on very high priced ground right next to Beverly Hills and there were very few people interested in getting involved in Century City. That was only for the first few years.

A law firm leased the top two floors of the first office building. They wanted to lease the third floor down from the top too but only for a short period of time, because they were involved in a big case.

A very wise man offered to lease the third floor and sublease it to the law firm on a year-to-year basis. He signed a twenty-five-year lease with Century City developers, as the law firm did upstairs, so he could get a lower rate for the lease. It was a flat rate for twenty-five years.

He subleased that floor, an entire floor - approximately 20,000 square feet. *Several years ago he was getting $10 MORE per square foot from the same law firm.* They have never moved. That means this investor gets $200,000 a year on his sandwich lease position. Not a bad NOTHING DOWN deal!

A sandwich lease can help you control property, too.

EXAMPLE: You talk with the owner of a house advertised for lease. The property has been vacant for awhile and the owner has just cleaned and fixed it up. No money coming in but the mortgage payment is due each month anyway, he complains.

SOLUTION: To solve his frequent vacancy problem, you offer to lease the house for FIVE YEARS, if he'll take 10% off the monthly rent. He agrees.

Then you go one step further. In the course of your conversation, the owner complained about taking care of repairs on the house, trips back and forth to fix this and that. So you offer to take care of that problem, too. After a mechanical inspection, if you're satisfied that there has been only normal wear and tear on the structure and equipment, you'll guarantee to fix anything that goes wrong with the house during the 5- year period — for another 10% off the rent. He agrees to that too.

But you don't stop there. With all your time and money invested in the house over a period of 5 years, you would also *like an option to buy that house included in the lease.* How about an option to buy the house at today's price good anytime during the next five years? See how you can tie up a lot of future profit?

The only other clause that you want to make sure to add to the lease is that even though you're responsible for paying the rent, you have the right to sub-rent to other people that are approved by you. Why? Because now that you

Lease Options

knocked 20 to 25% off the market value rent, the next thing you do is run an ad in the paper, "House for lease."

What are you trying to do? You're trying to get a positive cash flow that you can put away, just in case there are fix ups and repairs. All you really want to do is break even. Why? Because you want five years of appreciation with no money down - an excellent technique to start your investment program.

Tips For Finding Lease Options

1. Look for "sellers" with low loan balances. The less they HAVE to pay out on loans, the less they will need to extract from you to break even.

2. Some investor/owners rent for a very cheap rent in hopes of avoiding vacancies or complaints. Some don't raise rents and don't do cosmetic fix up. Try offering the same low rent the former tenant paid. Point out that their cash flow won't be changed and now you'll be responsible for solving the owner's "passed over" problems. As a trade-off, here's where you might want to offer to do fix up and repairs in return for a low rent.

3. Look for people in a high tax bracket — especially those who are so successful they don't have the time to mess with management.

Pro Tenant Lease With Option To Buy

Following is the style of lease and option I use when I'm signing a lease rather than being the owner. It favors the tenant in most every way possible.

1. The lease is separate from the option.

2. The lease is assignable and can be sublet.

3. Lots of option money applies.

4. When the option is funded, *payments* are made rather than all cash.

The benefits go on and on, but you can read it to see. **Remember, IT'S PRO TENANT.**

The first lease option is completed; the second is a blank form for your use.

Chapter Eleven

OPTION AGREEMENT

THIS AGREEMENT made and entered into this 1st day of January, 19___ by and between Ole Harddeal and all title holders to the property (hereinafter referred to as "SELLER"), and Bernard Hale Zick (hereinafter referred to as "BUYER").

This Agreement is with respect to property commonly known as: 105 Oak, Dallas, Texas and legally described on attached Exhibit A, which is made a part hereof.

> **(NOTE: DOUBLE CHECK BOTH THE STREET ADDRESS AND "COMMONLY KNOWN AS" AND THE LEGAL DESCRIPTION.** This is *very* important. You could copy the legal description from the seller's deed.)

In consideration of the promises, the parties hereto agree as follows:

1.0 Consideration: In consideration of one hundred seventy five dollars ($175.00) per month paid beginning January 1, 19___ and other good and valuable consideration, SELLER grants to BUYER or assigns, an exclusive option to purchase the Property for the sum of Sixty two thousand five hundred dollars ($62,500) for the first thirty months from date of agreement and sixty five thousand dollars ($65,000) thereafter.

> **(NOTE:** ONLY THE MONTHLY AMOUNT PAID THAT IS APPLIED TO THE OPTION IS LISTED HERE. The amount due for rent is listed in the lease. Also, note that the right to assign the option is in here. This form calls for a price increase after 30 months. Get what you can.)

1.1 Term of Option: Said option shall be exercised no sooner than twelve (12) months after date of option nor later than sixty (60) months after the commencement of said option term. The exercise of said Option shall be evidenced by delivery of a thirty (30) day written election to exercise fully executed by BUYER, and delivered to SELLER within the prescribed exercise period.

> **(NOTE:** This seller has just bought the property and didn't want a sale for a year. Don't offer a 12-month duration if not needed. See "Notice of Option.")

1.2 In the event of the exercise of said option, it is understood and agreed that if any rent payments are received by owner during the term of this option, said rent payments shall not be applied against the purchase price. Only the $175 monthly option money referred to herein shall be applied to reduce the balance due seller in the event of exercise of option. In the event of a default of payments due under the option, all option payments (and/or any lease payments) will be forfeited and forever be the property of SELLER.

> **(NOTE:** In this paragraph, we wanted to make sure the default in the lease was not tied to a default in the option and to soften this by pointing out that the option payment was not refundable.)

1.3 Loan Information: Attached to and made a part hereof is a schedule of loan(s) which are filed as a lien(s) against the Property at date of this agreement. Seller hereby warrants that no other valid liens exist nor will additional liens be placed against the property during the option period. BUYER may assume said loans at time of exercise of option should lender so permit, paying the balance due SELLER, (the difference between the loan(s) and option exercise price), in one hundred twenty (120) equal monthly amortized payments together with interest at ten percent annual rate.

Lease Options

> **(NOTE:** Not only should the loans be listed clearly and fully in the schedule, with current amount due, to whom, (with address), loan number, recording information, etc. Make sure you READ the notes and mortgages for unusual clauses or to see if the loan actually gets *larger* over time. Also, note the prohibition against future borrowing. Lastly, here's where we slip in the automatic owner carried financing upon purchase.)

2. The prompt payment of the option payment is a major consideration in the owner's granting this option. Default shall be defined as option payments being made thirty (30) or more days late. Acceptance of any late option payment is an automatic waiver of default.

> **(NOTE:** THE LAST SENTENCE IS IMPORTANT TO YOU.)

3. Exercise - Real Estate Contract: In the event of the exercise of said option, the sale of the property from SELLER to tenant shall be evidenced by a warranty deed and closed as per a standard form Real Estate Contract as officially adopted by local Realtors as set forth in Exhibit "B."

4. SELLER Has Title: SELLER represents that he has a bona fide contract in good standing or is in title to the Property and it is not now in default on any liens thereon. SELLER to provide BUYER proof of title and satisfactory loan status prior to this agreement's date of commencement or BUYER may void this agreement and any other agreement concerning BUYER, SELLER, and this property and all monies will be refunded to buyer. Said proof to be to the satisfaction of BUYER. In addition, SELLER agrees to immediately forward to BUYER a true and correct copy of any notice sent to him by any lender or the owner with respect to any defaults on this Property and where possible, approve lender sending duplicate notices directly to buyer. A notice of "equitable interest" shall be signed and filed at signing of option.

> **(NOTE:** The notice of equitable interest may be called a "Notice of Option" or a "Notice of Agreement." Your choice. But remember, many loans prohibit leases or options of more than 3 years, so be careful with what you file. If a "clause 17 - due-on-sale" exists, the more ambiguous the notice, the better.)

5.0 All notices and payments required or permitted to be given to BUYER or SELLER hereunder shall be delivered as follows:

BUYER:	SELLER:
Bernard Hale Zick	Ole Harddeal
Box 630	2229 Vine
Solana Beach, CA 92075	Fort Worth, TX 76140

5.1 Notice of change of address shall be given in writing.

6. LOAN DELINQUENT: Should SELLER be delinquent on any payment due under the first note and mortgage outlined in the attached, or any other lien of record against the property on date of signing this option, BUYER may, at BUYER'S option, make such payment and receive two dollars ($2.00) credit towards purchase of subject property for every $1.00 expended.

> **(NOTE:** Go for $4 for every $1, if you can do it!)

7. LOAN DEFAULT: Should SELLER cause any note and mortgage outlined in the attached listing of liens to be foreclosed upon, or notice of foreclosure filed, then BUYER may at his

discretion cure the default and pay SELLER one hundred dollars ($100.00) for SELLER'S entire remaining equity as a full and complete purchase price to the seller and the difference that would have been due is waived as full and complete liquidated damages in that exact damages would be difficult if not impossible to calculate. The seller will execute a recordable general warranty deed as then specified and in so doing waive any and all redemptive rights.

NOTE: We have strong language concerning the owner letting the loans on the property lapse. While this may appear severe to some readers, it is important to remember that it is the seller who is violating the terms of the agreement, guilty of rendering what you felt you were obtaining less valuable (if not down-right unobtainable) and who is causing the distressful situation. However, this point is one to discuss with your attorney. You don't want it to be so strong it gets tossed out.

8. SELLER shall not further encumber, nor do anything to permit any encumbrance on this property during the term of this agreement.

9. During the term of this option SELLER shall insure the property against physical damage, casualty etc. for SIXTY TWO THOUSAND FIVE HUNDRED DOLLARS ($62,500) for the first thirty (30) months and SIXTY FIVE THOUSAND DOLLARS ($65,000) thereafter, plus additional amounts as indicated by property value increases. BUYER will be named in the policy "as an additional insured, as his interest may appear." IN WITNESS WHEREOF, the parties have signed this Agreement the day and year first above written.

by:_____ Date: _____
    OLE HARDDEAL
    SELLER(S)

by: _____ Date: _____
    BERNARD ZICK
    BUYER

STATE OF _____)
)
COUNTY OF _____)

On this_____ day of _____ , _____ , before me, a Notary Public, personally appeared _____ and _____ who executed the above and foregoing instrument their _____ and acknowledged that they executed the same as their free act and deed.

IN WITNESS WHEREOF, I have hereunto set my hand and affixed my seal the day and year first above written.

_____

LEASE AGREEMENT

THIS LEASE made this first day of January, 1984 by and between Ole Harddeal as the owner of the Property located at 105 Oak, Dallas, TX hereinafter referred to as the "Property," said owner hereinafter referred to as "Landlord," and Bernard Zick of Solana Beach, California hereinafter referred to as "Tenant."

WITNESSETH:

Landlord hereby leases to Tenant (for occupancy and use as a private dwelling and storage of tenant's personal property, and no other purpose whatsoever except as allowed by Dallas, Texas Zoning), creating a sixty (60) month tenancy, unless terminated as hereinafter provided, for the sum of TWENTY FOUR THOUSAND DOLLARS ($24,000.00), beginning on the first day January, 1984, payable in equal monthly installments of FOUR HUNDRED DOLLARS ($400.00) each, to be in the office of Landlord IN ADVANCE OF the 1st day of each calendar month during the lease term.

Payments will be delivered or mailed to:

_____

and if tenant chooses for any reason to be late, a late charge of 5% will be imposed as of 4 p.m. on the 15th of the month.

The parties hereto further agree as follows:

1. Care of Premises: Tenant has inspected the property and acknowledges it is in a good clean condition. Tenant shall take good care of the leased premises, fixtures and appurtenances thereto, and keep them in good repair, free from filth, overloading, danger of fire, explosion or nuisance, and return the same to Landlord at the expiration of the term, in as good condition as when received by Tenant, reasonable wear and use, damage by fire or other casualty not caused by negligence of Tenant, his family, guests or servants excepted. Tenant agrees to hold Landlord harmless from any liability arising from injury to person or property caused by any act or omission of Tenant, his family, guests, servants, assignees or subtenants.

2. Alterations: Tenant will not, without Landlord's written consent, make any major alterations in the leased premises and will not deface or permit the defacing of any part of the leased premises. Tenant shall comply with insurance regulations regarding fire, lightning, explosion, extended coverage and liability insurance; and nothing shall be done or kept in or on the premises by Tenant which will cause an increase on the premium for any such insurance on the premises or on any building of which the premises are a part or on any contents located therein over the rate usually obtained for the proper use of the premises permitted by this Lease or which will cause an increase of the premium for any such insurance on the premises or on any building of which the premises permitted by this Lease or which will cause cancellation of any such insurance; and Tenant further agrees to comply with all city ordinances and the laws of this state and to save Landlord harmless for or on account of all charges or damages for non-observance thereof.

3. Assigning or Subleasing: Tenant shall have the right to assign, transfer or encumber this Lease or any part thereof, with written notice to Landlord and shall have the right to sublet or allow any other tenant to come in with or under Tenant. The undersigned Tenant shall, however, remain personally liable for damage done by any such future tenants.

4. Rules: Tenant will observe and comply with such reasonable rules as Landlord may prescribe from time to time on written notice to Tenant for the safety, care and cleanliness of the property. A true and correct copy of the current rules if any, are attached.

5. Utilities: Tenant shall furnish and pay for all electricity, gas, fuel, and other services used in or assessed against the leased premises.

6. Damage by Casualty: In the event of damage to the leased premises by fire, explosion, providential means or any other casualty, without the fault of Tenant, and if the damage is so extensive that it cannot reasonably be repaired within thirty (30) days after the date of such damage, then at the option of tenant the term hereby created shall terminate as of the date of such damage and rent shall cease as of such date on the condition that Tenant forthwith surrenders the premises to Landlord. In all other cases where the leased premises are damaged by fire or other casualty without the fault of Tenant, Landlord shall have the option to terminate this Lease by giving written notice of his intention to do so within five (5) days after such casualty, or Landlord, at his option, may elect to repair the damage with reasonable dispatch, and if the damage has rendered the premises untenantable, in whole or in part, there shall be an apportionment of rent until the damage has been repaired. In case of such damage, whether this lease is terminated or not, Tenant shall remove all of the rubbish and debris of Tenant property within five (5) days after written request by Landlord and, if this Lease is not thereby terminated,
Tenant shall not do anything to hinder or delay Landlord's work of repair and will cooperate with Landlord in such work. Landlord shall not be liable for inconvenience to Tenant by making repairs to any part of the premises or building, nor for the restoration of any improvements made by Tenant, nor for the restoration of any property of Tenant.

7. Eminent Domain. If the leased premises, or any part thereof, are taken by virtue of eminent domain, this Lease shall expire on the date when the same shall be so taken and return shall be apportioned as of said date. No part of any award for the leased premises, however, shall belong to Tenant.

8. Landlord's Liability. All merchandise and property in or about the leased premises shall be at Tenant's sole risk, and Tenant does hereby, now and forever, release Landlord from any claim for damages, howsoever caused. Landlord shall not be liable for damages or injury to any person occurring within the leased premises, unless proximity caused by or resulting from the negligence of Landlord, its agents, servants, or employees in the operation or maintenance of the leased premises.

9. Default. If (a) there be default in the payment of any rent when due and continuing for fifteen (15) working days thereafter, or (b) there be default in any other of Tenant's obligations hereunder, and if any such default or condition, then in either such event, (a) or

(b), Landlord may, at Landlord's option, at any time thereafter while such default or condition continues upon proper legal process, declare this Lease terminated and enter upon and repossess the premises, as aforesaid. The Landlord then, as agent of Tenant, may relet the same for the balance of the term of this Lease, or for a shorter or longer term, and may receive the rents therefore, applying the same, first to the payment of the expenses of such reletting, including brokerage, cleaning, repairs, and decorations, and then to the payment of rent due and to become due by this Lease and performance of the other covenants of Tenant as herein provided; and Tenant agrees, whether or not Landlord has relet, to pay to Landlord the rent and other sums herein agreed to be paid by Tenant, less the net proceeds of the reletting, if any, as ascertained from time to time, and the same shall be payable by Tenant on the days above specified for the payment of rent. If any such default be other than for non-payment of money and it would take more than fifteen (15) working days to cure the same, Landlord shall not terminate this Lease or enter upon the premises for such default if Tenant begins to cure such default within fifteen (15) working days and proceeds with the cure therefore with due diligence to completion. Tenant shall pay to Landlord the amount of any reasonable legal or attorney's fees if Landlord must take legal action to compel performance by Tenant of his obligations hereunder or any legal action in connection with Tenant's tenancy hereunder.

10. Fixtures. All repairs, affixed improvements, alterations, additions, installations, permanently installed equipment and fixtures, by whomsoever installed or erected shall belong to Landlord and remain on and be surrendered with the leased premises as a part thereof at the expiration of this Lease.

11. Waiver. A waiver by Landlord of any default hereunder for a period of sixty (60) days shall be construed to be a continuing waiver of such default or breach, but not as a waiver or permission, express or implied, of any other or subsequent default or breach.

12. Notices. Any notice to Tenant required by law, lease or otherwise shall be sufficient if delivered to Tenant sent by first class mail, postage prepaid, to Tenant at the Property or at a post office box should tenant so designate in writing subsequent to signing this lease. Any notice of intention to vacate, or any other notice from Tenant to Landlord, shall be in writing and delivered personally to Landlord or delivered to:_____ , Landlord's agent.

13. Landlord's Right of Entry. With a forty-eight hour notice, Landlord or Landlord's agent may enter the premises at reasonable hours to examine the same and to do anything which Landlord may deem necessary or advisable for the good of the premises or any building of which they are a part; and within one (1) month before the termination of this Lease, Landlord may display a "For Rent" sign on the premises and show same to prospective tenants. If Tenant(s) shall not be personally present to permit any such permissible entry into the premises, Landlord may enter same by a master key, without being liable in damages therefore and without affecting the obligations of Tenant hereunder.

14. Representation. Landlord has made no promise to alter, repair, decorate or improve the premises, but represents the condition and repair of the premises to be in good workable

order, except as are set forth herein. Neither party has made any representation or promises, except as contained herein. Tenant liability for rent shall not commence until possession is given or the leased premises are available for occupancy by Tenant. No such failure to give possession shall in any way affect the validity of this lease. Lack of notice to Landlord of needed repairs within 20 days of Tenant's entry into possession of the leased premises shall be conclusive evidence that the lease premises and the building of which it is a part are in good and satisfactory order and repair at such time.

15. Successors. The provisions, covenants and conditions of this Lease shall bind and inure to the benefit of the heirs, legal representatives, successors and assigns for each of the parties hereto, except that no assignment, encumbrance or subletting by Tenant without written consent of Landlord shall vest any right in the assignee, encumbrancer or sublessee of Tenant. Landlord shall be released from and Landlord's grantee shall be liable for, all liability of Landlord hereunder accruing from and after such grant of the revision.

16. As a material inducement to Tenant to perform under the term of this lease in a prompt manner, without delays whatsoever, Tenant will be given an option to purchase subject property. During the first twelve (12) months of occupancy, should tenant be in default of any payment due longer than thirty (30) days, in addition to the normal remedies under this Lease, the option will be null and void forevermore, and Landlord will keep all rent and all option consideration as full liquidated damages for all claims (except the cost of physical damage to the property) in that actual damages would be difficult if not impossible to ascertain, and all parties will hold each other harmless.

_____
LANDLORD

_____
TENANT

OPTION AGREEMENT

THIS AGREEMENT made and entered into this _____ day of _____, 19___ by and between _____ and all title holders to the property (hereinafter referred to as "SELLER"), and _____ (hereinafter referred to as "BUYER").

This Agreement is with respect to property commonly known as: _____ _____ and legally described on attached Exhibit A, which is made a part hereof. In consideration of the promises, the parties hereto agree as follows:

1.0 Consideration: In consideration of _____ dollars ($____.00) per month paid beginning _____ ,19___ and other good and valuable consideration, SELLER grants to BUYER or assigns, an exclusive option to purchase the Property for the sum of _____ ($__ , ____) for the _____ months from date of agreement and _____ dollars ($___,000) thereafter.

1.1 Term of Option: Said option shall be exercised no sooner than _____ (___) months after date of option nor later than ____ (___) months after the commencement of said option term. The exercise of said Option shall be evidenced by delivery of a_____ (___) day written election to exercise fully executed by BUYER, and delivered to SELLER within the prescribed exercise period.

1.2 In the event of the exercise of said option, it is understood and agreed that if any rent payments are received by owner during the term of this option, said rent payments shall not be applied against the purchase price. Only the $___ monthly option money referred to herein shall be applied to reduce the balance due seller in the event of exercise of option. In the event of a default of payments due under the option, all option payments (and/or any lease payments) will be forfeited and forever be the property of SELLER.

1.3 Loan Information: Attached to and made a part hereof is a schedule of loan(s) which are filed as a lien(s) against the Property at date of this agreement. Seller hereby warrants that no other valid liens exist nor will additional liens be placed against the property during the option period. BUYER may assume said loans at time of exercise of option should lender so permit, paying the balance due SELLER, (the difference between the loan(s) and option exercise price), in _____ (___) equal monthly amortized payments together with interest at ____ percent annual rate.

2. The prompt payment of the option payment is a major consideration in the owner's granting this option. Default shall be defined as option payments being made_____ (___) or more days late. Acceptance of any late option payment is an automatic waiver of default.

3. Exercise - Real Estate Contract: In the event of the exercise of said option, the sale of the property from SELLER to tenant shall be evidenced by a warranty deed and closed as per a stand-standard form Real Estate Contract as officially adopted by local Realtors as set forth in Exhibit "B".

4. SELLER Has Title: SELLER represents that he has a bona fide contract in good standing or is in title to the Property and it is not now in default on any liens thereon. SELLER to provide BUYER proof of title and satisfactory loan status prior to this agreement's date of commencement or BUYER may void this agreement and any other agreement concerning BUYER, SELLER, and this property and all monies will be refunded to buyer. Said proof to be to the satisfaction of BUYER. In addition, SELLER agrees to immediately forward to BUYER a true and correct copy of any notice sent to him by any lender or the owner with respect to any defaults on this Property and where possible, approve lender sending duplicate notices directly to buyer. A notice of "equitable interest" shall be signed and filed at signing of option.

5.0 All notices and payments required or permitted to be given to BUYER or SELLER hereunder shall be delivered as follows:

BUYER: SELLER:
_____   _____

_____   _____

5.1 Notice of change of address shall be given in writing.

6. LOAN DELINQUENT: Should SELLER be delinquent on any payment due under the first note and mortgage outlined in the attached, or any other lien of record against the property on date of signing this option. BUYER may, at BUYER'S option, make such payment and receive _____ dollars ($_ .00) credit towards purchase of subject property for every $_ .00 expended.

7. LOAN DEFAULT: Should SELLER cause any note and mortgage outlined in the attached listing of liens to be foreclosed upon, or notice of foreclosure filed, then BUYER may at his discretion cure the default and pay SELLER_____ ($____) for SELLER'S entire remaining equity as a full and complete purchase price to the seller and the difference that would have been due is waived as full and complete liquidated damages in that exact damages would be difficult if not impossible to calculate. The seller will execute a recordable general warranty deed as then specified and in so doing waive any and all redemptive rights.

8. SELLER shall not further encumber, nor do anything to permit any encumbrance, on this property during the term of this agreement.

9. During the term of this option SELLER shall insure the property against physical damage, casualty etc. for _____ DOLLARS ($\_\_\_\_\_) for the first _____ (\_\_\_) months and _____ DOLLARS ($_____) there after, plus additional amounts as indicated by property value increases. BUYER will be named in the policy "as an additional insured, as his interest may appear."

IN WITNESS WHEREOF, the parties have signed this Agreement the day and year first above written.

by:_____ Date:_____
   SELLER(S)

by:_____ Date:_____
   BUYER

STATE OF   )
)
COUNTY OF   )

On this _____ day of _____, _____ , before me, a Notary Public, personally appeared _____ and _____ who executed the above and foregoing instrument their _____
_____ and acknowledged that they executed the same as their free act and deed.

IN WITNESS WHEREOF, I have hereunto set my hand and affixed my seal the day and year first above written.

_____

MY COMMISSION EXPIRES: Notary Public

_____

Chapter Eleven

LEASE AGREEMENT

THIS LEASE made this first day of _____ , 19___ by and between _____ as the owner of the Property located at _____ hereinafter referred to as the "Property", said owner hereinafter referred to as "Landlord", and _____ of _____ hereinafter referred to as "Tenant".

WITNESSETH:

Landlord hereby leases to Tenant (for occupancy and use as a private dwelling and storage of tenant's personal property, and no other purpose whatsoever except as allowed by _____ Zoning), creating a _____ (__) month tenancy, unless terminated as hereinafter provided, for the sum of _____ ($_____ .00), beginning on the _____ , 19___ , payable in _____ installments of _____ DOLLARS ($_____) each, to be in the office of Landlord IN ADVANCE OF the 1st day of each calendar month during the lease term.
Payments will be delivered or mailed to:

_____ , _____ , _____

and if tenant chooses for any reason to be late, a late charge of __ % will be imposed as of ____ p.m. on the ____ of the month.

The parties hereto further agree as follows:

1. Care of Premises: Tenant has inspected the property and acknowledges it is in a good clean condition. Tenant shall take good care of the leased premises, fixtures and appurtenances thereto, and keep them in good repair, free from filth, overloading, danger of fire, explosion or nuisance, and return the same to Landlord at the expiration of the term, in as good condition as when received by Tenant, reasonable wear and use, damage by fire or other casualty not caused by negligence of Tenant, his family, guests or servants excepted. Tenant agrees to hold Landlord harmless from any liability arising from injury to person or property caused by any act or omission of Tenant, his family, guests, servants, assignees or subtenants.

2. Alterations: Tenant will not, without Landlord's written consent, make any major alterations in the leased premises and will not deface or permit the defacing of any part of the leased premises. Tenant shall comply with insurance regulations regarding fire, lightning, explosion, extended coverage and liability insurance; and nothing shall be done or kept in or on the premises by Tenant which will cause an increase on the premium for any such insurance on the premises or on any building of which the premises are a part or on any contents located therein over the rate usually obtained for the proper use of the premises permitted by this Lease or which will cause an increase of the premium for any such insurance on the premises or on any building of which the premises permitted by this Lease or which will cause cancellation of any such insurance; and Tenant further agrees to

comply with all city ordinances and the laws of this state and to save Landlord harmless for or on account of all charges or damages for non-observance thereof.

3. Assigning or Subleasing: Tenant shall have the right to assign, transfer or encumber this Lease or any part thereof, with written notice to Landlord and shall have the right to sublet or allow any other tenant to come in with or under Tenant. The undersigned Tenant shall, however, remain personally liable for damage done by any such future tenants.

4. Rules: Tenant will observe and comply with such reasonable rules as Landlord may prescribe from time to time on written notice to Tenant for the safety, care and cleanliness of the property. A true and correct copy of the current rules if any, are attached.

5. Utilities: Tenant shall furnish and pay for all electricity, gas, fuel, and other services used in or assessed against the leased premises.

6. Damage by Casualty: In the event of damage to the leased premises by fire, explosion, providential means or any other casualty, without the fault of Tenant, and if the damage is so extensive that it cannot reasonably be repaired within_____ (___) days after the date of such damage, then at the option of tenant the term hereby created shall terminate as of the date of such damage and rent shall cease as of such date on the condition that Tenant forthwith surrenders the premises to Landlord. In all other cases where the leased premises are damaged by fire or other casualty without the fault of Tenant, Landlord shall have the option to terminate this Lease by giving written notice of his intention to do so within____ (__) days after such casualty, or Landlord, at his option, may elect to repair the damage with reasonable dispatch, and if the damage has rendered the premises untenantable, in whole or in part, there shall be an apportionment of rent until the damage has been repaired. In case of such damage, whether this lease is terminated or not, Tenant shall remove all of the rubbish and debris of Tenant property within_____ (__) days after written request by Landlord and, if this Lease is not thereby terminated, Tenant shall not do anything to hinder or delay Landlord's work of repair and will cooperate with Landlord in such work. Landlord shall not be liable for inconvenience to Tenant by making repairs to any part of the premises or building, nor for the restoration of any improvements made by Tenant, nor for the restoration of any property of Tenant.

7. Eminent Domain. If the leased premises, or any part thereof, are taken by virtue of eminent domain, this Lease shall expire on the date when the same shall be so taken and return shall be apportioned as of said date. No part of any award for the leased premises, however, shall belong to Tenant.

8. Landlord's Liability. All merchandise and property in or about the leased premises shall be at Tenant's sole risk, and Tenant does hereby, now and forever, release Landlord from any claim for damages, howsoever caused. Landlord shall not be liable for damages or injury to any person occurring within the leased premises, unless proximity caused by or resulting from the negligence of Landlord, its agents, servants, or employees in the operation or maintenance of the leased premises.

9. Default. If (a) there be default in the payment of any rent when due and continuing for _____ (__) working days thereafter, or (b) there be default in any other of Tenant's obligations hereunder, and if any such default or condition, then in either such event, (a) or (b), Landlord may, at Landlord's option, at any time thereafter while such default or condition continues upon proper legal process, declare this Lease terminated and enter upon and repossess the premises, as aforesaid. The Landlord then, as agent of Tenant, may relet the same for the balance of the term of this Lease, or for a shorter or longer term, and may receive the rents therefore, applying the same, first to the payment of the expenses of such reletting, including brokerage, cleaning, repairs, and decorations, and then to the payment of rent due and to become due by this Lease and performance of the other covenants of Tenant as herein provided; and Tenant agrees, whether or not Landlord has relet, to pay to Landlord the rent and other sums herein agreed to be paid by Tenant, less the net proceeds of the reletting, if any, as ascertained from time to time, and the same shall be payable by Tenant on the days above specified for the payment of rent. If any such default be other than for non-payment of money and it would take more than_____ (__) working days to cure the same, Landlord shall not terminate this Lease or enter upon the premises for such default if Tenant begins to cure such default within _____ (__) working days and proceeds with the cure therefore with due diligence to completion. Tenant shall pay to Landlord the amount of any reasonable legal or attorney's fees if Landlord must take legal action to compel performance by Tenant of his obligations hereunder or any legal action in connection with Tenant's tenancy hereunder.

10. Fixtures. All repairs, affixed improvements, alterations, additions, installations, permanently installed equipment and fixtures, by whomsoever installed or erected shall belong to Landlord and remain on and be surrendered with the leased premises as a part thereof at the expiration of this Lease.

11. Waiver. A waiver by Landlord of any default hereunder for a period of _____ (__) days shall be construed to be a continuing waiver of such default or breach, but not as a waiver or permission, express or implied, of any other or subsequent default or breach.

12. Notices. Any notice to Tenant required by law, lease or otherwise shall be sufficient if delivered to Tenant sent by first class mail, postage prepaid, to Tenant at the Property or at a post office box should tenant so designate in writing subsequent to signing this lease. Any notice of intention to vacate, or any other notice from Tenant to Landlord, shall be in writing and delivered personally to Landlord or delivered to: _____ , Landlord's agent.

13. Landlord's Right of Entry. With a forty-eight hour notice Landlord or Landlord's agent may enter the premises at reasonable hours to examine the same and to do anything which Landlord may deem necessary or advisable for the good of the premises or any building of which they are a part; and within one (1) month before the termination of this Lease, Landlord may display a "For Rent" sign on the premises and show same to prospective tenants. If Tenant(s) shall not be personally present to permit any such

permissible entry into the premises, Landlord may enter same by a master key, without being liable in damages therefore and without affecting the obligations of Tenant hereunder.

14. Representation. Landlord has made no promise to alter, repair, decorate or improve the premises, but represents the condition and repair of the premises to be in good workable order, except as are set forth herein. Neither party has made any representation or promises, except as contained herein. Tenant liability for rent shall not commence until possession is given or the leased premises are available for occupancy by Tenant. No such failure to give possession shall in any way affect the validity of this lease. Lack of notice to Landlord of needed repairs within __ days of Tenant's entry into possession of the leased premises shall be conclusive evidence that the lease premises and the building of which it is a part are in good and satisfactory order and repair at such time.

15. Successors. The provisions, covenants and conditions of this Lease shall bind and inure to the benefit of the heirs, legal representatives, successors and assigns for each of the parties hereto, except that no assignment, encumbrance or subletting by Tenant without written consent of Landlord shall vest any right in the assignee, encumbrancer or sublessee of Tenant. Landlord shall be released from and Landlord's grantee shall be liable for, all liability of Landlord hereunder accruing from and after such grant of the revision.

16. As a material inducement to Tenant to perform under the term of this lease in a prompt manner, without delays whatsoever, Tenant will be given an option to purchase subject property. During the first _____ (__) months of occupancy, should tenant be in default of any payment due longer than _____ (__) days, in addition to the normal remedies under this Lease, the option will be null and void forevermore, and Landlord will keep all rent and all option consideration as full liquidated damages for all claims (except the cost of physical damage to the property) in that actual damages would be difficult if not impossible to ascertain, and all parties will hold each other harmless.

_____
LANDLORD

_____
TENANT

Lease Options For Positive Cash Flow

We have discussed options for the control of future appreciation, and lease options to cover a negative cash flow. Now, to the "fun" correlative, that opportunity to get a positive cash flow through lease options.

In the Chapter which includes "Options As a Geographical Asset," I will discuss a sale leaseback, but here's a similar situation, where the lease option brings positive cash flow.

EXAMPLE: A Kansas Savings & Loan went under. The state closed the doors. They made too many bad loans and were now in receivership. I knew about several of the properties in question. Various attorneys, bankers and others had told me about the S&L before the general public knew.

The third day after a receiver was appointed, I was at their door. I knew that among the properties involved were ten houses in a suburban town. I offered $275,000 for all ten of them, with the seller (the S&L) to give 75% loan-to-value ratio loans on each, at a favorable interest rate.

They signed the contract. I included "and or assigns" on the line stating the name of the buyer. I intended to sell each of these houses to investors. Total commissions would be $19,250.00. The houses were a good buy, at about $32,000 each, but I could not qualify for ten loans. But the commission looked good and I knew the investors I had in mind would let me share in the profits. Right then I was equity rich and cash poor!

This project was southwest of Kansas City and most of my investors were from California. They all knew each other and sent one person out to drive by the houses. The two thousand mile distance wasn't a worry to them. (They wanted no part of property management even if the properties were next door!)

I signed a lease for five years on each house. The rent was about $210.00 per home per month — just enough to pay for principal and interest. I was also to pay all taxes, insurance and upkeep.

I upped the rents to nearly $250 per month. This is known as a sandwich lease. I rented (with option) at $210 and sublet at $250, giving me a positive cash flow.

Six months later I was contacted by the person who owned the land behind the houses. HE wanted to buy the same houses because he planned to build a retirement center and wanted to start the project with those houses.

I had an option to buy the houses at $32,000 each. They were now worth that amount, up to $35,000 each. The developer paid *me* $2,000 per house for the option to buy the houses at $37,500 each. The option was for 18 months. And, he leased them from me at $250 per month plus maintenance. This way, I increased by positive cash flow to about $20 per house, (no management, no maintenance headaches). He took care of all problems. Technically, this was an option on my option, sort of a sandwich option.

His lease with me might be called a master lease, in that he leased all 10 houses.

Don't forget, I had $20,000 cash for the option and more to come if he bought.

Over 18 months he got rents up to an average of $285 per house. They rose in value to $40,000 each. But, he never got a loan to build the retirement home and never exercised the option. I got the ten houses back with an average $45 per house positive cash flow. I raised rents to $325 for a total $850 per month positive.

A year later I ran short of cash again, so I sold the houses to an investor for $35,000 cash. He liked the low price, (since they were worth $42,500 by then), because it made the deal low risk. In return, you guessed it, he gave me a lease at $210 per month, as I had before and an option at $37,000.

Since my original option was at $32,000 and he bought at $35,000, I picked up an additional $30,000.

Now, that's $70,000 I've gotten out of the deal so far and my positive cash flow is over $1,000 per month!

There's more to the story, but you've learned the main lesson.

1. I bought right for my "partners" so my option had value.

2. The leaseback gave me potential cash flow.

3. The sublease and double options let me realize that cash flow.

4. Options = cash flow & control!

Also remember these points. If you own a house or any rental property, you can increase your cash flow by adding an option to the lease. This is true for free and clear properties as well as leveraged ones.

If you lease option a property, you can get a positive cash flow by leasing it to users at a higher lease rate. And, if you want, you then could lease option to the sub-tenant!

Lease Option Pitfalls

There is one problem with the lease option. As advised, and for maximum profit, you should make the length of the option run as long as possible. Five years is usually the maximum amount of time that you could reasonably expect a seller to accept.

However, now YOU ARE LOCKED IN to a five-year lease, and that may be a problem. I speak from experience.

I held a five-year lease option on a $200,000 property. I paid $10,000 for the option, but got most of that back in special requests for property modifications that I wanted done.

The lease payment was ridiculously low for the first year and a little over market at the end of the fifth year.

The option price, $200,000 - which was top of the market - but market for the time we got the option.

After three years, I moved from Overland Park to the San Diego area. The sublease tenant paid $400/month less than I had paid. The monthly lease was 50% below market for what a buyer had to pay but this was in the fourth year and remember, lease payments increased each year.

Worst of all, the value was down to about $175,000. This was due, in part, to market softness. The main reason was due to the widening of a nearby street, about seven years ahead of schedule!

Now the real problem, the sublease, (with a super tenant), ran out six months before the lease! (The potential negative from the sublease and vacancy was nearly $25,000.)

After lots of hard negotiations, I paid about $6,000 to the owner who, 1) got my improvements, 2) got the option canceled, 3) got direct control over the tenant and in return, released me from the lease.

How can you profit from my loss? What do I intend to do the next time?

How about this? "I'll lease your place for a year, (or 18 months), but if I pay on time and I'm not in default for any other reason, and take care of all minor maintenance problems myself, I want an option to buy the property thereafter and a one year renewal of my lease at the same rate."

"Furthermore, I want the option and the lease, under the same conditions and to have two more renewals if I decide to stay."

In this case, the landlord has the benefit of your option and your renewals being subject to timely rent payments. You get to measure the merit of the investment every 12 or 18 months, to see if you want to continue. Both parties win. You might want to use this idea as an owner too!

Chapter Twelve

Selling Lease Options

It is possible to sell property once you've leased-optioned it. It's unusual to be able to sell something you don't own, but in the technique we'll use, you only partially sell it, just like you partially own it. The advantage for this sort of transaction is that properties are usually leased-optioned for less per month than they'd be sold for on a dollar received per month basis if the money paid were interest. A technical way of describing this is to say the gross rate multiplier is less than the loan constant.

Although the legal issues are quite simple, this isn't the ordinary way of doing things. To get somebody to go along with this concept, you'd probably have to be working with a motivated home seller and an anxious home buyer.

Lease-option is a claim against the equity in a house. The claim is a simple one. The option is a contractual right, as we discussed, to acquire title to the real estate. It is like a claim against the equity. If recorded, it is not only a claim against the equity, it is a lien against the title.

There is a method of selling properties known as a "Contract for Deed." You may know it as a land contract or land sales contract. It seems every third state has picked a different name for it. I like to call it a contract for deed because you sign a contract that says that if you make the payments, you'll get the deed.

The contract for deed approach offers enough benefits to warrant its use in many situations. You should be aware also of some of its potential difficulties:

    a. eviction proceedings may be more complex since optionee is not just a tenant

    b. the ownership of improvements and responsibilities for damage need to be spelled out

    c. the ability of either party to lien the property needs to be clear

d. what rights in the property can be sold or transferred and by whom

   e. disposition of the property if owner dies before option is exercised

   f. can prepaid monies be retained by seller in case of default

   g. applicability of home office tax deductions to optionee

   h. standard forms are difficult to find

The key to this entire arrangement is that you say to the person you're selling to, "if you deliver the money, I can DELIVER the deed." It doesn't say that you have the deed, it just says that you can deliver the deed. If you have an option to purchase a piece of property, then you have the right to acquire the deed.

If you have an option to purchase a house you can sell that house on contract for deed on the assumption of the contract for deed. We would have to assume that the option would expire either on the same date as the contract for deed or it would run a little longer. Furthermore, we assume that there are no qualifying conditions to the option that would limit the exercise of the contract for deed. If there was a qualifying condition in the option, then you would have to put that same qualifying condition in the contract for deed. What we're looking to do here is to pass through the optioned rights to the contract for deed holder.

We're going to use a somewhat exaggerated example to get the point across.

EXAMPLE: A house is available for $300,000.00. It is located in a large metropolitan, midwestern city, and is in the "upper bracket" category. It probably would have sold long ago, but at this point in time there is a credit crunch. Loans are very difficult to obtain and the interest rate seems high compared to last year. The sellers have asked for all cash and their unimaginative agent never thought to ask them whether or not they'd help in the financing. The answer would probably have been no on the day she took the listing, but now several months have passed and the house still has not sold.

You approach the owners with the concept of a lease-option. You point out to them that with the lease-option they'll be able to depreciate their house, thus giving them some tax shelter. You want to sign a long-term lease. Because of the fact that you are willing to take care of all maintenance and management problems, you'd like a rental rate of $1,400.00 per month instead of the usual $1600.00 to $2,000.00 a month that might be due for this property.

After long negotiations they finally agree. You then run an ad in the paper for a $330,000.00 house for sale, 10% down and 10% interest. Because of the extremely low down payment and the extremely low interest rate relative to other fixed rate loans available on the market, four prospective buyers want to see the property. You take them by the house that you are about to lease-option

Selling Lease Options

and, so as to gain access, explain that you have advisors, friends and relatives that you want to show the property to.

One of the people agreed to purchase the house. You explain to them that the transaction's quite simple. They give you 10%, which is $33,000 at closing and, in addition, make monthly interest payments to an escrow account that you are going to set up. Because they will own the house, they will naturally pay for the taxes and insurance and do all maintenance. You are giving them a three-year term on the ten percent financing. They must refinance at the end of three years. You point out to them that the market for loans should be much better by then and they can refinance earlier if they so wish.

On the other side of the transaction you tell the people who own the property that you want them to put a deed in escrow with the escrow company handling the transaction. You're also willing to sign a quit claim deed that says that should you fail to make your lease option payments of $1,400.00 per month, that the quit claim deed may be recorded.

If the buyer does a title search as arrangements are made to close these two transactions, he will be concerned that you don't have title to the property. The answer's very simple. You will explain that you haven't recorded the deed, but will have it in time to complete the transaction. The buyer will sign the contract for deed and make all payments to the escrow company. A deed from the current title holder to you will be also placed into escrow as well as a deed from you to the buyer. If the buyer ever comes in with the $297,000, both deeds will be handed to him for recording.

The instructions on the option say that the option price is $300,000 and you've paid $3,000 as option consideration and that money is to apply towards purchase. The balance due on the option is $297,000. The option is good for the next 40 months. This way you have a four-month leeway to market the house to somebody else in case the current contract for deed buyer fails to close. (This also means that you have the obligation to pay four months of rent, but remember at closing you're going to have a lot of cash.)

At the closing, the contract for deed purchaser will put up $33,000 cash. Three thousand of that you'll use to purchase the option; $30,000 is your profit. I've made the assumption here that the house has a range of value that would allow it to be sold for $330,000 on terms. (Let me have my assumption for now in that the example would still work if you didn't have such a range on the value of the house and if you took less money as the down payment on the contract for deed.)

The monthly interest payments will be $2,470.00. Compare this to a rental payment of $1,400.00 and you'll have a handsome monthly cash flow. As you can also see by this example, there are a lot of different ways the numbers can still work out. Given how much you're receiving per month on interest, you

Chapter Twelve

could reduce the interest rate and increase how much you pay for rent and still have a good deal. You could use 9% interest and 9% down and pay $1,600 a month rent and still have a heavy cash flow.

How well this transaction will work depends on many different things. Lower priced houses in expensive areas like San Francisco, San Diego and parts of the greater New York area rent for a great deal of money. For instance, if you can find a house for $130,000 in an older area of San Diego, you can rent it for $900 per month. If the house happens to be in one of those prized older areas, you might get as much as $1,100.00 per month. Whereas, in the midwest a $130,000 house is more likely to rent for $750 to $850 per month.

The amount of money received per month in rent divided by the value of the property is called the gross rent multiplier. The gross rent multiplier used to be universally one percent. If you have a $60,000 house, you get $600 per month. This has changed dramatically in different parts of the country.

One of the factors that makes this entire transaction, is that the gross rent multiplier gets worse as the price of the house goes up. Conversely, it gets better as the price of the house goes down. This is the reason that beginning investors are often advised to buy lower priced properties. They are more "efficient." Efficiency in this case means that the less you pay for the house, the more money you get in rent per dollar paid for the house.

For instance, if you had a $100,000 house that would rent for $1,000 per month, in the same neighborhood you would find that a $200,000 house would rent for $1,700 and a $400,000 house would rent for $2,900. You'll note as the amount of money you pay for the house goes up, the rent goes up more slowly.

The loan constant is the number of dollars paid per period divided by the amount of the money due at the first of the period. If you're paying an interest only loan, the loan constant is equal to the interest rate. The loan constant in this case is ten percent annually.

It would seem logical that this technique works best on higher priced homes. The higher the price of the home, the less the rent and therefore the bigger the spread between rent and interest payments. However, it can be used quite successfully on lower priced homes.

Chapter Twelve

Part Four

Long Term Profits

Chapter Thirteen

Zero Interest Financing

An Option Is Better Than A Loan

People have various motivations for agreeing to sell an option. Sometimes the people are very influential and have many real estate investments. *They look at the option as a no-frills and no problem way of disposing of a property.*

More than likely, the "seller" of the property doesn't want to or *can't obtain a loan to solve his cash flow problems and the pure option seems like a viable alternative.*

Following are some situations that would call for this approach.

EXAMPLE: Her husband died 15 years ago and she's been working as a bookkeeper since. She is past retirement age and only because of the benevolence of her employer, has she been allowed to stay on for so long. She has a part-time job as a babysitter, but because of her advancing age, she fears that source of money may disappear. She knows that she can continue babysitting for another two years and her small mortgage will be paid off. However, the taxes, insurance and small amount of maintenance that she has to hire out is more than she can handle. She's thought about applying for a loan because the equity is so high in her home, but at age 72 it's hard to find a lender.

SOLUTION: You offer her a pure option. You will pay for her taxes and insurance plus $25 a month toward the maintenance bill, for an option to buy the house. The option lasts as long as she lives. You set the price at a fixed amount so that the longer she lives, the better it is for you. Thus, you don't mind paying option consideration off into the future. When she dies, you can exercise the option.

EXAMPLE: He had a very good job. His hourly pay could be attributed to his union status and his seniority. But because of increasing union demands for higher pay, despite the non-inflationary economy, the company went out of business. He spent six months looking for jobs at the old pay schedule and found none. Three months later he did get a job, but it paid a lot less than he was used to receiving. Not only is he on a tight budget now, he can't pay for back payments and he is seriously in arrears. Foreclosure is filed at the courthouse steps and the sale is scheduled for two weeks AFTER he starts his new job. Because he's behind, his creditors run. He called you because he heard you sometimes lend money on real estate.

SOLUTION: You then offer him a pure option. You offer him an option to buy a half interest in his house, at far below what the house would be worth today. You only get an option to buy half the house because you want him to be financially involved with the future of this house. If you asked for an option to buy the entire house, he might not take care of it - so that would depreciate the value. By getting a bargain price on half the house, he knows that the value of the other half of the house *will come to him* at the time of sale.

EXAMPLE: She has worked hard to earn the money to buy her house. She put an illegal apartment in the basement. With hard work, her job income and extra cash flow from downstairs, she's always done well. Now she has the bug to write a novel. She sent an initial script to her publisher who said her book would be accepted. They even gave her a small advance. Now she won't be able to work overtime and that means no extra money and that means that the downstair's rent and her current income aren't enough to cover her payments. She'd do most anything to get her shot at being an author.

SOLUTION: You offer her a pure option. You'll give her a number of dollars, enough to make sure her mortgage is paid for the next two years, for the right to buy her house at the end of two years. She figures to be a best selling author by the end of two years and gladly signs the documents. The option is low and all the option money will apply toward purchase. YOU BOTH GET WHAT YOU WANT.

EXAMPLE: She wanted a chance to have a career. She got tired of her husband saying that all she did was "take care of the kids and anybody could do that." She took a college course prior to filing for the divorce but the transition time and expenses of being on her own were more than she could really handle. She got the house and the two kids, but her new high tech sales job allowed for tremendous bonuses for performance with a relatively small base pay. Sure, she's going to do well in the future. But she doesn't want her first major act as a single woman to be the loss of her house - the home for her children! She considers borrowing the money, but what if she can't make it at this job — and does she want to take the risk? Besides, a woman who has two teenagers to support and only one month on the job is not a prime loan applicant.

SOLUTION: You Offer Her A Pure Option.

EXAMPLE: She used to joke about her income as "pen" money. That was until she lost her job. Now this couple doesn't have enough to cover the mortgage payment. Neither of them realized how important her job income had been to the family for the past 15 years. They don't want to sell the house, especially because their daughter will be a senior in high school the following year. Perhaps the best bet is to get a loan. Even though there is a large equity in the house, he has been very good at using credit cards and living the full American dream — whether earned or not. He doesn't qualify for a loan under anybody's standards because his debt to retailers exceeds his equity. They could move to a smaller house but not until the daughter is out of school and the wife is not too anxious to go back to work either.

SOLUTION: Just when all other avenues led to a dead end, your offer to option the house for 18 months seemed the perfect solution. You offer appraised value less 10%, (tell them you have to have a bargain), less costs of the commission. (There are no commissions. You just ask for another 7% off because if *they* sold in 18 months, *they'd* have to pay one.) The option price is good for 18 months and you'll give them all cash at the time of exercising the option. They chomp at it.

Options: A Better Way To Finance Properties

For quite a few years now, financing has been the determining factor in real estate purchases. Is is available to you? Do you have to "qualify" for the financing and can you do it?

Even when the affordability index, (index maintained by the National Association of Realtors which shows the average person's ability to borrow in relationship with the loan necessary to purchase the average residential property), hit the best numbers for years in the period from 1986 to 1988, many people couldn't qualify for the specific property they wanted to purchase.

Yes, interest rates were down during that period, and more people made enough money to qualify for a loan. However, many would-be homeowners still couldn't qualify, especially if they were interested in assuming the loan on a property with a high interest rate loan that was placed on it in the 1978 through 1983 period, when 12%- 16% loans were not uncommon.

Furthermore, just the uncertainty of your ability to finance a real estate transaction can often weaken the deal.

EXAMPLE: A seller has a very prime piece of property. It's fairly priced and well located. Two buyers submit offers on the same afternoon. Buyer No. 1 has shaved $8,000 off the asking price and is offering all cash with no contingencies. That buyer has lined up financing and knows that the money is readily available. AND he has a lot of cash to put down. (Anytime you have 25% cash to put down, financing becomes pretty simple.)

Buyer No. 2 thinks he may qualify. Maybe this buyer has had some problems with credit in the distant past or part of his income is from an outside job that isn't consistent. For whatever reason, he needs to enter into some kind of an acquisition agreement wherein his ability to finance the property is one of the conditions.

If Buyer No. 2 is going to offer the same total number of dollars in cash, he has three basic options. Let's explore them.

First, that buyer can sign a normal real estate purchase agreement and say that the contract is "subject to the buyer obtaining financing acceptable to the buyer." If I were going to write that kind of a subject to clause, that's how I'd phrase it. I would want to make sure that the contract was subject to financing and financing that I approved. You could just say, "subject to buyer obtaining financing," I suppose that's safe enough. There is a potential risk that the seller could line you up with a source that would give you the loan but on terms that you couldn't sleep with.

In either case, "subject to" financing, even if you say "subject to buyer obtaining a loan with interest rates of 12% or less and fully amortized over 30 years," or some such thing, you have a standard real estate contract with a standard "subject to financing" clause. If you, as buyer No. 2, have offered the exact same number of dollars for the property as Buyer No. 1, it's a foregone conclusion that Buyer No. 1 will get the contract.

There is a second approach to making an offer on a standard real estate contract. You could avoid disclosing to the seller that you don't have the financing and need to obtain it. **Instead you could state in the contract that the earnest money deposit, (the money you put up when you sign the contract), is forfeited should you not close.**

You, of course, will need to qualify for financing. If you don't find the loan, you will lose your earnest money deposit and that's all. This is known as a **liquidated damages clause**. *This effectively turns a real estate contract into an option but you are not being nearly as honest with the seller.* Besides that, earnest money deposits are usually held for a closing that will take place in a short period of time.

The third approach is to use an outright option to purchase the property. There are several advantages to this. One advantage is that sellers will usually give you longer periods of time with an option than they will with a purchase agreement that needs to be closed. Options are usually considered for a 3 to 9-month period of time or even years. The time before closing is usually anywhere from 30 to 90 days at most.

Yes, you probably will have to put a little more money down on an option than you would with earnest money, but you have a lot more control and therefore more time to go out and find the financing.

You will lose the earnest money and you'll lose the option money if you can't finance the property. And you may have to put up more option money than earnest money. **But you'll be able to buy more time**. Time is the crucial factor in finding financing.

If the dollars are the same and Buyer #1 offers cash and you ask for an option, who will win? That depends. Remember, option money isn't taxed when received. If the option money is enough and the length of time *carries the close into another tax year, the seller may prefer the option.* If the option is six months or more, you may feel that the flexibility it offers you is worth offering a figure closer to the full purchase price. In which case, some sellers would choose your deal. And besides, some sellers start to sell long before they *really* want to move. A firm option offer with a delayed close date may be just the ticket, where a "subject to loan approval" contract would be turned down quickly.

Secondly, an option can be superior to a "subject to" because sellers sometimes use "subject to's" to wiggle out of contracts. I recall a case reported to me back in 1978, when prices of housing in California were going up at an unbelievable pace. It was not uncommon for a house to increase in value by $10,000 to $15,000 between the time the seller agreed to sell and the date of closing! If the time to close involved a month or two, sellers would sometimes use a "subject to" clause to wiggle out of the contract.

In one case, a buyer said his purchase was subject to approval for a VA loan. The contract allowed him enough time to get the approval. It took six months for the VA loan to be granted. The buyer decided to skip it. In the meantime, he was approved for a conventional loan and didn't want to finish doing the paperwork for the VA. The buyer came forward saying he was ready to close and he had a conventional loan. Using the "subject to" as an out, the seller said he was going to sell to somebody else. Within a flash the seller sold the property for $15,000 more to another party.

It never pays to try to sue on contracts. At least rarely. In this case, the buyer found out from his lawyer that the seller did have a "leg to stand on." The buyer had agreed to get a VA loan and had not done so. So as you can see, sellers use "subject to" clauses to wiggle out of contracts just as well as buyers.

Thirdly, **the quality of your transaction will improve if you have more time to find the financing**. Yes, you can probably find a decent loan within 30-60 days for most standard real estate purchases. But if you put money up as an earnest money deposit, and you really do want to buy the property, you will probably take the first loan that you qualify for.

With a little longer term option, you'll have the time to shop around and get the best loan possible. One of the biggest downfalls of real estate ownership today is owning properties with negative cash flows. *If you don't have the time to shop for financing, how can you be expected to optimize your investment situation.*

It might be easy to grab an adjustable rate loan because buyers qualify for those more readily than they can a fixed rate loan. There are two problems with this. If you rush in to an adjustable rate loan, you might get one that has terms and conditions you won't be able to live with later. The next interest rate adjustment could put you in such a negative cash flow situation that you lose the property.

ARM loans differ in maximum interest rates charged, or caps, as they say. If you rush to obtain financing, you probably won't do a complete job of analyzing the terms of the loan in question. Loan availability changes too. Funds may be plentiful one week but the market dries up two or three weeks later. The smaller the community, the more often this is true.

Adjustable rate mortgages, also called variable rate loans, are those loans in which the interest rate varies over time. The amount of the increase/decrease in interest rate is usually tied to the cost of money, the general cost of living index or determined by the terms of the loan itself. The amount of the change in interest rate is determined, as is the frequency of the change, by the terms of the loan. In addition, the total amount of the change is also limited by contract. Some contracts call for the changes to be reflected in the payments, in full or part, and some have them tacked on to the end of the loan.

Lenders have funds available in large blocks, available at certain interest rates or under certain terms and conditions. If the market interest rate changes slightly, there is always a delay before approval can be given for changing terms. If the interest rate improves for the buyer, loan money gets snapped up and there isn't any available. Terms for the borrower may get worse. It takes a certain amount of time and paperwork for lenders to say exactly what their new rates are going to be. And, with so many influences on the availability of capital in the United States, especially with government borrowing, there are short periods of time that loan money just isn't plentiful.

If you sign on a contract to buy which is to close within 90 days, you don't have a lot of time to sit around and wait for loans to become available.

Anxiety builds as one looks for the funds to close. We all have become emotional about purchases. The more we want a property, the less we are able to negotiate skillfully. We may **become a short term borrower** to solve an interim financing situation. If you have good lines of credit, your banker will quite often "float a loan." These short term loans usually "float," (there's that word again), at a few points above prime.

Too often, these short term loans become long term loans. If you are floating three points over prime, it's not much different than floating three inches under ice. You'll end up like Houdini, having to float down the river motionless — with your nose pressed against the ice, gasping for air in that half inch space that's left between water and ice!

Chapter Thirteen

Zero Interest Financing

It doesn't sound like fun, does it? **Real estate is a long term investment and if you are buying long term you should finance long term**. An option will help you avoid the temptation to borrow short term for a long term purchase. **Lastly, an option can help you profit from a property when you may never be able to (or want to) qualify for financing.** We'll explore that concept next.

Options To Avoid Loan Qualifications

You could use a renewable option to avoid qualifying for a loan. If the option money applies, and you can talk the seller into a long enough option, you could always keep the property under option for your entire holding. If you intend to keep the property for 3-7 years before you sell it, just keep rolling it over for 3-7 years.

Eventually you could have the property paid for or maybe, after that long a period of time, the seller would be willing to provide financing for you. You could attempt to make this a condition of the option.

We made this a condition in the option we use. Read paragraph 1.3 in the Pro Tenant Lease Option (Chapter 11). That last sentence converts the option to owner financing at the end of the option period. To negotiate this clause into your option, just point out to the seller that if you continue to make option payments in a timely manner over such and such a period of time, that you have proven yourself to be a person worthy of financing.

Not all optionors will agree to this particular provision. However, if all of the other terms are more than satisfactory to the owner, we have found this to be an acceptable arrangement in many transactions. If the owner does not agree, you may want to adjust some of the other terms of the agreement.

The most dynamic use of an option as a financing tool that will allow you to avoid having to qualify for a loan, is that of a **double closing**. If you have an option to purchase a piece of property but only intend to sell this property to another at a higher price, **you can advertise and sell the property to somebody else who can qualify for the loan.** If your option to purchase the property is on terms of all cash to the seller, and you don't have the down payment or the cash but you can tie up the property with an option, you have to find somebody who can finish the transaction.

Run an ad in the paper stating that you have the property for sale, but only work with those buyers who have down payment money and sufficient credit to qualify for a loan. When you find one, your problems are solved.

Work with the escrow officer at the escrow company, or title policy company, or your attorney, depending on what part of the country you're in.

EXAMPLE: If you live in the northeast United States, go to your lawyer and show him your option terms and conditions. He will help you draw up the contracts to sell the property to your new buyer. Your option price is $100,000 and you're selling price is $120,000. Rather than qualifying for a loan yourself

Chapter Thirteen

and then turning around and selling it to the new buyer, have the new buyer qualify for a loan based on the $120,000 sale's price. That's the legitimate price that he will be paying for the property and he will have to be able to qualify accordingly.

If he does, the lawyer can take his purchase proceeds and use those monies to fund your option. You have, in fact, bought and sold the property without ever having to go into title!

The same would hold true in this situation if you were working with a sophisticated buyer. You could sell the option to the buyer, (or trade it), and take your profit that way.

If you have the option to buy a house for $100,000 and it's worth $120,000, then the option is worth $20,000. You can cash in on your profit without ever having to qualify for a loan. You could sell the option for $20,000 or perhaps trade it for something worth $20,000 to you.

Beginning investors should rethink this idea several times. It's a very realistic way of getting started if you lack money and/or sufficient credit.

Options Are Zero Interest Loans

We have said it elsewhere in the text, but let's just make sure you understand one of the most potent values of an option.

Option to buy - zero interest loan

In effect, an option is a zero interest loan. If I have an option to buy your property for $50,000 and that option is good for five years, then I really have a five year, zero interest loan. I don't owe you any more money at the end of five years than I do at the begin beginning of five years. The principal balance, the amount necessary to exercise the option, stays constant.

If the option price went from $50,000 to $55,000 over a five-year period of time, I suppose you could say that we paid "10%" interest over five years. That's still not too bad a rate.

Lease With Option To Buy Zero Interest Loan

If you sign a lease with option to buy and the amount that you pay in excess of the normal rent rate is applied toward the purchase price, you have a zero interest loan with principal only payments. If you can get the lease with option to buy extended again and again and again, even if you pay more and more money every month towards principal, you're still getting a zero interest loan with the principal only payments.

EXAMPLE: You've financed a property on a lease option for three years. Some of the option money has been applying toward purchase, as option consideration. For example, you have been paying $600 per month with $100 per month as option consideration. Normal rent would have been $500. The $100 applies to reduce the purchase price which is constant.

At the end of three years, you are unable to qualify for financing. You failed to include a clause in your option agreement that allowed for automatic financing. When you see the end of the option is near, you approach the seller to reaffirm that he really doesn't want the property back. He is comfortable with the cash flow that you have been giving him but he is not renewing at a fixed option price. In fact, he isn't very anxious to renew!

Why not tell him you will pay $900 per month if he will extend the option for another three years. However, rather than $100 applying toward purchase, (which was the case of the $600 monthly payment level), you want $400 per month to apply toward purchase. He is liable to snap it up because of the increased cash flow. Point out that you are giving him the extra money in return for the fact that he is extending the option as is. This way the price stays constant. **You have now picked up a three-year zero interest loan.** Yes, stop to think about it. The price doesn't go up and the option money applies, you are actually getting credit toward the principal without paying any interest. If you can extend this again, all the better!

Why wait to get this approved if you're now going out to negotiate a new option? In the initial option, use the increased monthly payments as an inducement to get the seller to extend the option term past what he would have initially.

EXAMPLE: The seller seemed to be willing to give you a three year lease with option to buy at $600 per month. He's even pushing for five years or longer. Toss your hands in the air and tell him you give up, he wins! You'll just have to pay him $900 per month for the 37th through the 72nd month so that you can convince him to extend the option as far as you want it. If he goes for it, you've even got a better deal because you've extended your time past what he originally agreed to and you're still in zero interest financing. You know, you might be able to let the price that you pay for the equity in the property go up a smidgen in a situation like this!

Options As A Financial Aid To Sellers

Since options are such a flexible tool, they can be used to solve a great number of problems. Sellers can benefit from some of the aspects of option financing too.

EXAMPLE: The seller has a good piece of property but he is in poor health. The property has experienced tremendous appreciation and future appreciation is almost guaranteed. To make his life simpler, the seller would prefer to sell today but at tomorrow's price. The solution would be to finance the eventual sale of the property with an option.

SOLUTION: Let's assume the property is worth $200,000 today and will be worth $500,000 in five years. The seller could seek out an aggressive builder-developer who would gladly sign to buy the property for $400,000 with the option being good for five years. Or, should he so decide, the seller could make the option price at $300,000, further guaranteeing that the option will be exercised.

Now the seller doesn't have to worry about being around to market the property to the point of its eventual sale. With the option being advantageous, the buyer is pretty sure of exercising.

Here is a more vivid example, however, I can't image a duplication of this situation.

EXAMPLE: I once obtained an option to buy a piece of land from a seller who was afraid that his heirs would never sell it properly. He sold me the option to buy the property at a bargain price. He was in good health at the time he was involved in the option and didn't know if he would be in the future. He knew that I would have to buy the property under the terms and conditions of the option and his estate's executors wouldn't have to negotiate any further.

To put the icing on the cake, he had me use my option money to buy life insurance. Yes, I bought insurance on his life that was funded to a trustee in the event of his death. Should he die during the option, the option money was given to the trustee to be used for me to buy the property under the option. Thus, he knew for sure that if he died during the option period, his estate would have cash.

The premium for the insurance clause seemed quite steep. It was a little steeper than what I normally would have paid for the option. There was definite value to the insurance policy and the benefits that could come from the funding of that policy.

Needless to say, you'd never want to make someone of questionable character the beneficiary of an insurance policy on your life! However, in this case I did buy the property under the option and the seller outlived the option. And in fact, is still around and may outlive all his heirs! (For more on options and estate freezing, read the section titled "Options and Estate Freezing" in Chapter 10, Tax and Financial Planning.)

Here is another seller advantage of an option. Many sellers want their holdings kept quiet. To put a For Sale sign on the property saying that you own such and such an office building and you want to sell it, tells the entire world who owns it.

If you list a property very few people know who owns it, but as negotiations go on and on, more and more people know.

If you could just sell the property to an individual on a quick cash sale, no one would need to know who the beneficiary of the sale was. But such private sales are hard to come by.

By selling an option to the most likely buyer, you don't have to work with real estate brokers and inform them of your ownership, nor do you have to put a sign on the property. I have always referred to someone with an option as a **"silent salesman."** The world need not know that the person who holds the option is trying to get money to develop the property or to buy the property so that the owner gets cash in his pocket. As an option holder, you can do most of your exploratory financing and attempts at reselling the property acting as if you do own the property. **Properly structured, an option could give the seller a high degree of confidentiality**.

A broker friend of mine in Wichita also used the option to assist him in *negotiating as well as financing* his purchase for a piece of property. In this particular case the sellers couldn't agree on anything.

EXAMPLE: The sellers were two elderly sisters and both of them wanted to make sure that they sold their half interest in the property for a higher price than their sister. No one could get both of them to agree on a listing agreement or a sale's contract.

My frustrated broker friend, who wanted to buy the property for his own account, finally approached both the ladies on the same day with this proposal.

"I will go to each of you in a one-day period of time and sign an option to purchase your half interest in the property. Each of you will negotiate independently of the other and I won't inform either of you what the other has agreed to sell for. In fact, neither one of you will ever know what the other person sold for unless you want to tell each other."

"If I have a firm option from each of you to buy a half interest in the property, then I'll know what I have to pay ultimately for the whole property. You won't have to deal with each other, you'll just have to deal with me. Since I have an option, I'll have enough control to go out and get my financing. I will be more than happy to put a clause in each option agreement that I cannot buy one half of the property at a time. If I'm to buy the property at all, it has to be both halves purchased at the same time."

This ended up being a successful technique for dealing with parties who would not talk to each other sanely. The two prices ended up being very close to each other and the buyer didn't have hours or days of negotiating squabbles.

I have taught this technique to various students who have used it successfully in working with feuding partners in a syndication. By having a strongly drawn option, you have control over the property one part at a time. There is no "subject to" somebody else's approval and each person's confidentiality can be maintained.

Chapter Thirteen

Chapter Thirteen

Chapter Fourteen

Control And Other Uses

Motive: No Profit, Just Control

EXAMPLE: I'm dealing with somebody on a piece of property I really need to control. I'd like to hold the option at the flat price. But if having control of ownership is important, even without profit, I could take an option to buy their property at whatever it's worth at the time I buy it.

This is quite often the case with companies that want to own the property next to them in case they want to expand. They don't mind paying what the property is worth in the future. *They just want to make sure they can buy it.*

EXAMPLE: A friend of mine in St. Louis owned a warehouse dock and knew he'd need to expand someday. I suggested he option the adjacent property at market value just to avoid the cost for relocation in the future. He didn't mind paying appraised value for the piece next door. He just wanted the control - to know that during the next 10 years he, and only he, could buy it when he needed it — for what it was worth. And since the seller *refused* to sell for less than appraised value, we at least made sure no one else would buy the property and force my friend to move when he expanded.

Avoiding Ordinary Tax On Quick Sale Of Options

You can sell an option on your option. This would be especially advantageous to you if you held an option for a short period of time and wanted to get capital gains treatment on the option.

EXAMPLE: You have a one year option to buy a piece of property. You have held the option for one month and someone else falls in love with it. He wants to buy the property and is willing to close sometime during the next eleven months. Your option is perfect for him because it has eleven months to run.

However, if you sell today you'll have short term capital gains, which is the same as ordinary income. You could always give him an eleven-month option to purchase your option. He would give you, let's say, $19,000 today with another $1,000 due at the time you transfer the actual option to him. You have solved your tax consequences.

Even if there were no tax advantages, an option on an option is still a viable way of pulling profit out of an option without having to qualify for a loan.

EXAMPLE: You have an option to purchase a piece of property for $100,000. You have gone through the process of having the land zoned. The property is now worth $200,000 and you still have another year to go on your option. *There is $100,000 profit in that option.*

Another person wants to buy the property from you. He doesn't have the cash to buy it today and he needs to qualify for financing, (but you know he can't). He is willing to pay you $35,000 today for the option to buy your option so that he can get the property ultimately. This $200,000 piece of property is worth $500,000 to him if he can get financing and building permits, etc.

He seems like your most likely prospect and since you only put up $10,000 to get the option in the first place, the $35,000 will show you a tidy profit of $25,000, even if all else fails. Thus you can sell an option to purchase the option and see if he can carry through.

If you're smart, you'll try to negotiate a shorter period with him than the time you have left on your option. Thus, if you have twelve months left on your option, you'd sell him an option for ten months giving you two months left to sell it to somebody else. You, of course, would be following his progress very closely and wouldn't bother with lining somebody else up to buy the option if he was next to closing. However, if he starts dropping the ball halfway through, you could get somebody else to step in. Or, you could sell a second option to buy the option, (which is subject to the first option to buy the option not being exercised).

Options & Due-on-sale

A common misconception is that options avoid the "due-on-sale" clause that is found in many mortgages and deeds of trust today. Lenders include that clause so that if you transfer the property to another person, the lender has the right to call the loan. This gives them a chance to bring the interest rate up to market or refuse the new title holder assumption of the loan because of bad credit.

A second common misconception is that options will NOT AVOID a "due on sale" clause. The true answer is "it depends."

Too many people take a real estate broker or a loan officer's word for *whether there is* a "due on sale" clause in a deed of trust or mortgage and whether or not it is *enforceable.* This is ludicrous. People make honest mistakes while others might lie for their own benefit. Many savings and loan employees will automatically tell you, "Yes there is an enforceable due-on-sale clause in that mortgage," even though they've never read the document! It's just a good standard answer for them to give.

Chapter Fourteen

Several times I have been told that there was an enforceable "due-on-sale" clause but found that there wasn't when I read the document myself.

On two occasions I purchased properties from sellers who told me a "due-on-sale" clause was enforceable. I bought the properties after reading the documents and assuring myself that there WAS NOT an enforceable "due-on-sale" clause at all. I never agreed with the seller nor did I feel a need to tell him of my discovery. Because of the owner's firm belief that the loans were not assumable, I was able to negotiate a fairly advantageous purchase price. After closing, I confronted the lender with the fact that the "due-on-sale" clause in one case wasn't there and in the other case wasn't enforceable, and, in both cases, I was able to step in and take over the loans.

The lesson here of course is to read the "due-on-sale" clause.

Some of the older "due-on-sale" clauses have this sort of wording: "In the event of transfer of the deed, the lender has the right to call this loan." This is a very weak "due-on-sale" clause. It has to do with transfer of the deed. If you buy on *contract for deed* or take an *option* to purchase that piece of property, this sort of "due-on-sale" clause may not be enforceable. If this is the case, the option can help you circumvent the due-on-sale clause. So, it is important that you read the documents and look at any such clause.

If clause 17 is included, there is little you can do.

Here is how clause 17 reads:

"Uniform covenant. #17. Transfer of the Property; Assumption. If all or any part of the Property or an interest therein is sold or transferred by Borrower without Lender's prior written consent, excluding (a) the creation of a lien or encumbrance subordinate to this Mortgagee, (b) the creation of a purchase money security interest for household appliances, (c) a transfer by devise, descent or by operation of law upon the death of a joint tenant or (d) the grant of any leasehold interest of three years or less not containing an option to purchase, Lender may, at Lender's option, declare all the sums secured by this Mortgage to be immediately due and payable. Lender shall have waived such option to accelerate if, prior to the sale or transfer, Lender and the person to whom the Property is to be sold or transferred reach agreement in writing that the credit of such person is satisfactory to Lender and that the interest payable on the sums secured by this Mortgage shall be at such rate as Lender shall request. If Lender has waived the option to accelerate provided in this paragraph 17, and if Borrower's successor in interest has executed a written assumption agreement accepted in writing by Lender, Lender shall release Borrower from all obligations under this Mortgage and the Note."

"If Lender exercises such option to accelerate, Lender shall mail Borrower notice of acceleration in accordance with paragraph 14 hereof. Such notice shall provide a period of not less than 30 days from the date the notice is mailed within which Borrower may pay the sums declared due. If Borrower fails to pay such sums prior to the expiration of such period, Lender may, without further notice or demand on Borrower, invoke any remedies permitted by paragraph 18 hereof."

(Since paragraph 14 and 18 are relevant to this due-on- sale clause, they are printed below.)

"14. Notice. Except for any notice required under applicable law to be given in another manner, (a) any notice to Borrower provided for in this Mortgage shall be given by mailing such notice by certified mail addressed to Borrower at the Property Address or at such other address as Borrower may designate by notice to Lender as provided herein, and (b) any notice to Lender shall be given by certified mail, return receipt requested to Lender's address stated herein or to such other address as Lender may designate by notice to Borrower as provided herein. Any notice provided for in this Mortgage shall be deemed to have been given to Borrower or Lender when given in the manner designated herein."

Non-Uniform Covenants. Borrower and Lender further covenant and agree as follows. Acceleration; Remedies. Except provided in paragraph 17 hereof, upon Borrower's breach of any covenant or agreement of Borrower in this Mortgage, including the covenants to pay when due any sums secured by this Mortgage, Lender prior to acceleration shall mail notice to Borrower as provided in paragraph 14 hereof specifying: (1) the breach; (2) the action required to cure such breach; (3) a date, not less than 30 days from the date the notice is mailed to Borrower, by which such breach must be cured; and (4) that failure to cure such breach on or before the date specified in the notice may result in acceleration of the sums secured by this Mortgage, foreclosure by judicial proceeding and sale of the Property. The notice shall further inform Borrower of the right to reinstate after acceleration and the right to assert in the foreclosure proceeding the non-existence of a default or any other defense of Borrower to acceleration and foreclosure. If the breach is not cured on or before the date specified in the notice, Lender at Lender's option may declare all the sums secured by this Mortgage to be immediately due and payable without further demand and may foreclose this Mortgage by judicial proceeding. Lender shall be entitled to collect in such proceeding all expenses of foreclosure, including, but not limited to, costs of documentary evidence, abstracts and title reports.

You'll notice that it prohibits any transfer of any equitable interest. Most people would consider an option a transfer of an equitable interest, but there is a lot of room for leeway.

For instance, you could have a 35-month lease and not be in violation of due-on-sale. If you went to the court house and recorded a memorandum of agreement concerning real estate, ostensibly to protect your 35-month lease, you would put a cloud on the title which, in some measure, would protect you, (the person who has the lease).

If you had a separate option to purchase the property that ran concurrently with the lease, and you decided not to disclose this option to any other party, you could, in the event of major problems, reveal the option that goes with the lease and perhaps protect your position.

Options As A Geographical Asset

Options can be used in a lot of other ways — such as a geographical asset.

EXAMPLE: I wanted to be involved in an office building in Dallas, Texas. (I'm also licensed to sell real estate in the state of Texas. I look at a lot of deals down there.) I was looking at a particular piece of property that I was really interested in when a fellow investor asked me to go into partnership with him.

I began to think that as a partner I would have to worry about maintenance, vacancies, and property management details.

SOLUTION: I told my potential partner that I'd give him $20,000 for an option to buy the property at such and such a price. That way he could use the cash to buy the property himself. He would run it and take care of it. I just wanted to have an option. That way I could have control of future profits without current responsibilities.

An option can be used as a geographical asset in another way. I've sold lots of Dallas and Kansas City houses to people outside of the area. How do I do that? I sell the houses to them, they put up enough of a down payment that the houses break even and then I lease the houses back, guaranteeing that they will continue to break even.

How long is my lease back? Usually three years which means even though I might lose a little bit of money the first year, I'll get a pretty good cash flow the second and third year. I usually get a right to renew the lease.

Why am I so generous as to sign a lease back guaranteeing a breakeven?

1. I get a commission when they buy the house in the first place - which is not bad, because it's usually the full commission.

2. I get the potential of cash flow.

3. I've got a little bit of control on the property because I'm taking care of it and managing it. If I want to exchange it or something like that, I can always call them up and they're right there.

Also, I get a lease back and an option combination that says I'm leasing the house back, guaranteeing a break even, but I have the option to buy that house with a nice little profit for them.

So if I do a good job of managing, bring good tenants in, really fix the place up and it blossoms in value, you get your money back plus a nice return, plus you don't have any worries, and I get paid for my efforts.

In fact, one of my clients said she came real close to complaining about a house she had purchased through me that I leased back. She said, "It took me a long time not to be nervous about this."

I asked why? She said that over the three years she received only three letters from me. I asked if that was at the end of the year with information she would need at tax time? She said, "Yes." The person that helped me put the deal together with her told her that this was the best kind of investment to have. I told her, yes, **that she had no idea how many phone calls she DIDN'T get** that my property management people and I DID GET concerning her little house that she owned.

That's the way you do it. That way the investor is completely passive. And the more sophisticated investors don't want to be bothered with a day by day report.

Why would you want to put so much time and work into it? Because, even though they own it, *you have an option for all the profits above a certain level.* And I've seen that add up to big dollars over time.

Chapter Fourteen

Chapter Fifteen

Equity Sharing Option

The Players / Their Roles

How has the option become an equity participation tool? First, let me cover some of the terms I use in equity participation so that you can easily follow.

There are three players on one side. Player #1 is the tenant, the straight, old, renting tenant, the tenant who pays you a monthly check. Player #2 is the tenant with option. Before we used to be owners and we'd rent to tenants and that was it and you had a positive cash flow. On later purchases you had a break even. If you were an investor making a purchase in the 1970's, you probably had a negative cash flow and you started looking at "selling" the tenant an option as a solution to the problem. You gave him that option to raise the amount you received from him so it was just a little bit more than straight rent.

In the late 1980's to 1990's we are looking at the tenant/buyer, the tenant that becomes a co-owner of sorts with you, and that's Player #3.

We potentially have three more players on the other side of the equation. On the other side we have the two equity investors and a cash flow investor. The first equity investor is the new buyer. I call him "A." Or, you could have a selling equity investor which you might want to call the owner carry-back equity investor. I call him "B." And, C is the cash flow investor.

Player #1 - Tenant

Player #2 - Tenant with option

Player #3 - Tenant/Buyer

A = Equity Investor (new buyer)

B = Owner-Carry Back Equity Investor

C = Cash Flow Investor

The buyer/tenant is somebody that is renting half the property and buying half the property. The (new buyer) equity investor is somebody who puts up equity money for a project but does not necessarily take over the negative cash flow. The selling equity investor is somebody who sells, but instead of getting all cash or carrying back a note, carries back an equity interest in the property. The cash flow investor is just that. That's the person who covers the negative cash flow.

All sorts of combinations are possible.

Many of these combinations involved passing the deed to the tenant — especially the ones that involve the tenant/buyer. But almost without exception, the same arrangements could have been done with an option to acquire the deed rather than a deeded interest. And, many legal experts will tell you the person with cash equity in the property (A's & B's) should be slow to deed over part interest in their investment property to a tenant. To them the option is a much more preferable alternative.

Many people are concerned about dealing with any kind of partners. They fear that, in the end, their partner will quote that part in the Bible where it says, "He was a stranger and I took him in."

I think it is more fun to make money with a partner than to do it by yourself. Many people agree with me. And I know these arrangements can be structured as a WIN WIN proposition.

Tenant With Option / Equity Participation

Now let's discuss the tenant with option. How can that be an equity participation?

EXAMPLE: Let's say you have a piece of property that you would like to buy. You have the money to put down. The rent would normally be $600 per month and the payments are $800 per month including property taxes, insurance and homeowner's fee. This might be the situation if you purchased the property recently and had put little or no money down. (I've seen "negative cash flows" worse than that, in fact.)

In this case you'd say to the tenant. "Would you like to be an owner?"

"Yes. I always wanted to own and have my own property, but I never could get the down payment together."

Your response could be "Let me check out your financial horizons, your past and future to see if you would make a good partner with me. If you check out, here's what I'm willing to offer you. If you'll pay $800 per month I will allow one-half of your monthly rent payment to apply towards purchase."

How is the purchase price derived? Get an appraisal or if there's a reasonable owner value that can be ascertained, we'll take today's price and you can buy half of the property at that price and the other half at whatever it's worth at the time you fund the option. Otherwise, what I'm doing is splitting the appreciation with you because you are not giving me a down payment. If it is worth $80,000 and it goes to $120,000 that's a $40,000 increase. I get the $80,000 plus $20,000 and half your monthly payment applies toward that.

Run some numbers. Every market is going to be different. Maybe you give credit for one-third of the rent. Maybe you use some other formula for allowed appreciation. It doesn't make any difference. Whatever fits your market. WHAT I'M TALKING ABOUT IS PUTTING SOME REAL TEETH IN IT AS A BENEFIT TO THE TENANT. You see? You want them as a partner and you want them as a partner for several reasons. The primary reason is if you buy a property with a negative cash flow, how many more can you buy? There's a limit isn't there?

If you buy a property with no negative cash flow, how many more like that can you buy? Ah! You can buy and buy and buy and buy, as creative as you are in acquisitions. That negative cash flow is going to run you out of business isn't it?

Now, how many of you like property management? How many people like to spend their Saturdays out showing an apartment when there's a good football game on? How about showing a single family house in Vail when it's a bright sunny day with 12 inches of new powder on the back bowl?

We don't like clean up, painting, vacuuming, shampooing the carpet, but we sure like the appreciation and that's the only reason we do it. It is for the tax benefits today, the savings of having a tenant pay down the loan and the appreciation. What we are willing to give is a little bit of appreciation. Because of the credit you are giving, you have no vacancy, no maintenance and no repair because you make that a part of the lease. Are you giving away too much? I don't know. Run some numbers. Do some projections. Find out. Stop to think.

Many investors will attribute the $400 first to the cost of ownership, then interest, and if any remains, to principal. Again, the costs of ownership are taxes, insurance and homeowner fees. If half of what they pay is applied to purchase of half of the house, then HALF the taxes, insurance and homeowner fee would be taken from the $400. Next, you subtract the normal market interest that would be due if they purchased half the house for nothing down. If any credit remains, that would go to reduce the purchase price.

If you had a #1, a plain old tenant in there, and it comes time to sell, is it easy to sell an occupied single family house? No. It is very difficult. Most buyers of single family houses are owner/ users that want to occupy the property so first you have to get the tenant out. The longer they have been in there and the less they have called you, the more you have to do once they leave. Right? Sometimes you have to replace the drywall behind the tiles in the shower before you put the tiles back in. If you're lucky you can match the tiles, or you come up with a very avant-garde pattern of tiles in your shower. You have to do all this work. When the tenant moves out you have repair, maintenance and you have replacement.

Who's paying the mortgage when that tenant moves out? I am. The owner. That's who's paying. So you have a negative cash flow. Then along comes the Realtor and he wants a commission. You add all this up and, gee, it might not be so bad having a person who sits in this house, has an option to buy, and one-half of the cash he pays per month is applied towards purchase. But, look at all the money you DON'T have to pay in.

Considering all this, giving the tenant $50-150 per month credit towards purchase is not too bad. Besides, if rent is normally $200 less than what they are paying, it really isn't your $200 anyway, is it?

Some people use this same program with a variation. As an inducement for the person to pay a higher amount, say $800 a month, you add: "If you don't buy I'll give you back $200 a month when you leave, so it's a savings program for you." I've seen situations where $100 a month was returned when the tenant left. That could add up to a lot of money and I don't know whether you want to put yourself into an agreement that you can't carry out.

With the HELP agreement we supply at the back of this text, you can pay out that $200 a month accumulation over several years! It is worth reading.

Basically you are getting an interest free loan. If the tenant moves out he gets all his cash back. In this flow of events you'd try to induce the tenant to think seriously about moving out and not funding on the option because you give him all the extra payments that he made. But you didn't owe any interest on it did you? You had no holding costs during this period.

There are many modifications and ways to vary the lease with option as an equity sharing tool.

Hopefully I have shown you that unusual combinations can be set up involving options, tenants and owners when the tenants are interested in owning.

More Lease / Option Opportunities

FOR INVESTORS: As investor you could do the same thing, couldn't you? If you didn't have money to put down on a piece of property, or if you didn't have a piece of property that you wanted to put into a program like this, don't you think you could go to somebody in this market, in this day and age and say, "Sir, I notice your house has been for sale for six months. Now I notice you are also running an ad in the lease with option to buy column. Might I assume that you are tired of the negative cash flow on this?"

"Yes."

"Have you had any good people ask about lease with option to buy?"

"Well, nobody seems to come up with the monthly payment I need."

Chapter Fifteen

Equity Sharing Option

"Here's what I'll do sir. For one-half the future appreciation in this property I will make the entire payment, lease this property and lease it back out to somebody else. Here are the other things that I want........"

No Negative Cash Flow With Lease / Option

In any market, there are people sitting on the edge of losing properties. Some people take advantage of this fact by offering this solution — they will cover the negative cash flow with a lease with option to buy agreement. "You want $100,000 for it? Good. I'll give it to you sometime in the next five years and in the meantime, I'll cover the negative cash flow that is causing you so much trouble." I've known deals to close just like that. You're covering maybe $100-$200 per month negative cash flow and you've got all that future appreciation.

Suppose the owner says no to your offer. Maybe you say that you'll lease and cover all the negative cash flow today and you'll buy at today's price plus half the future appreciation or some kind of combination. But, it's a true equity participation way.

What we're talking about again in equity participation is people taking uncommon roles. We used to have the owner who was a user, or the owner who is a landlord and the tenant, and then we have the lender. The owner owned and got all the equity benefits and all the write-offs. The tenant used and used cheaply but he got the use. The lender was paid a regular fee. And then the lenders noticed they had all these fixed dollar obligations outstanding coming back to them and they had fixed dollar obligations outstanding to the public. They were loaning you money for 30 years and then they were borrowing the money for five years to cover it and every five years the interest rate went up. It's like with Fanny Mae. Awhile back Fanny Mae had an average yield on their portfolio of 9% and an average cost of 10%. They had to do something. They had to get some kind of equity play.

Equity Participation Limitations

In all of my work with equity participation I have not found it to be a solution to over priced properties or properties with physical problems or bad investments. Equity participation is a way to group together people who allocate the responsibilities and benefits of the ownership of real estate toward their needs and abilities to pay. *This is not a way of moving over—priced properties.*

Buying Half A House

You could have a 3A, a tenant/buyer and equity investor/new buyer combination, couldn't you? You could have a 3B, tenant/buyer and owner carry back equity investor. A 3A would be when somebody buys a house with the idea that the tenant who's going to move in will get a half interest in the house for making the large payments necessary. "I'll put 20% down but you'll cover all the payments. I'm not going to just rent to you. I'm going to sell a one-half undivided interest in the house to you. Instead of paying $600 per month rent you'll pay $800 per month."

Some people have a problem with this as a concept. I think an easy way of looking at it is this way. I owned or you owned a duplex and it had two bedrooms

Chapter Fifteen

on each side of the duplex. One side had a large living room and a large kitchen. The other side had a very small living room and a very small kitchen. You come to me and you want to buy my duplex. Why?

"Well, I've got to have room for me and my family and my mother-in-law and uncle live with us."

I say, "Okay, that the duplex is $140,000."

"Oh! Oh! I was afraid of that. Can't afford that. What would the payments be on that?"

You figure it up and it's much, much more than they can afford. Well, how much can you afford?

"Well, I don't know. How much would the rent be on that?"

You say that, given the equity you have and everything else, the rest could be about $700 per side, or payments would be about $1,000 per side.

"I'll tell you what I can afford. I'll buy half and rent half. I buy half and live in it and pay you the $1,000 a month and rent half at $700 a month." Think of it that way for tax purposes and everything else.

Now, tear the duplex wall out of the center and you have equity participation. On the half that the #3 person is renting - that's rent. That's usually figured as normal market rent for the value of the house divided by two. The rest is allocated toward purchasing. You apply the purchasing money first to taxes, insurance, then to interest and if there's any left to principal. They're a home owner for the half they're buying. That's section 1034 of the Internal Revenue Code. That's buying a house.

Now for you, the investor, you've bought half the house and you own that as an investment and you rent it to them. On the half you own you get appreciation, depreciation and rent. On the half they're buying, they're just buying. It's really that simple.

THE DOCUMENTATION IS VERY IMPORTANT... how you outline this to make sure everything goes as it is supposed to, the old 50/50 all the way through. There are other programs such as tenants in common keeping equity together in which they do some different allocating. The investor puts 20% down, that's 20% of the property. They get 20% of expenses, the tenant gets 80%. I prefer the former approach, but your attorney's favorite way will probably dictate.

The basic concept here though is very simple. *If the rent for a house is so many dollars, the payments would be even more, and equity participation is somewhere in between.* The tenant/buyer has the advantage of no down payment and smaller monthly payments than normal to purchase. You, the

Chapter Fifteen

investor, have the advantage of a tenant that has an interest in the property, wants to take care of it, wants to maintain it, wants to do something with it and make it appreciate. The tenant covers all maintenance, all repairs, all fix up, all restoration.

Somebody asked me what I'd do if my tenant called and said they wanted to put in a $10,000 swimming pool. I'd say, "God bless you. Put it in right."

"Oh! You wouldn't help them pay for it?"

"No. I wouldn't. Not in my area of the country. A swimming pool is not going to increase the value of the property."

Now, if a tenant came in and said, "What I'd like to do is build a second bath in my one bath house."

I happen to know you get about $1.25 out of every dollar you invest when you have a 3-bedroom house with one bath and you put in a second bath.

I'd tell him maybe we could figure out something on that. Maybe I could give him some more money back when we sell. So you can modify the agreement after it is originally drawn. The original agreement says that the equity investor (A or B) who owns the property with the tenant buyer doesn't pay for any improvements. If the tenant/buyer (#3) wants to make any improvements, that's up to him and he has to pay for it. So you have an investment where you have no vacancy, no fix up, no maintenance, no worries, no hassles.

I talked to a lawyer who's helping me work on these equity participation agreements and he said, "I'll take about five of them. That sounds great. That's what I want. I want something totally passive. I want the depreciation. I don't want anything that will call me at night."

His concept is to buy a whole bunch of them and then every once in a while somebody is going to want to get out and he'll say, okay, let's put it on the market and sell. Then you split it 50/50.

The question is, if the tenant pays for extraneous improvements, as I refer to them, does he get his money back? No. Does this mean the tenant probably won't put in a pool? Yes.

If you want the tenant to put in a pool you've got a choice don't you? If you want you could say that you'll give him so much more money when you sell, if he puts the pool in. It's a business decision, but you don't want to structure the agreement giving the tenant the right to make improvements.

What about things like furnace, roof, air conditioner, and other repairs or replacements. The way I've always solved that is with HOW (Home Owner Warranty) insurance. I want to make sure I've got an insurance policy that will pay for all these major things breaking down. If you owned a piece of property

Chapter Fifteen

and the #3 was in after the 10th year of the home-owner's warranty insurance, suppose he came to you and said that the furnace just went out and he wanted you to go half? Don't you think you might be enticed to go half with him? Of course you would. If a hurricane came along and tore the roof off and the insurance company paid only 70% of it, do you think you would not pay the rest of it to get it done or go half with him.

So you can have a #3 and an A. You can have a #3 and a B. You could have a #3 to a B then an A.

One of the problems you are going to have if you get involved with the tenant form of equity participation is we don't look coordinated. The people that want to buy on equity participation have found their dream house and the seller wants all cash. The seller that wants to sell on equity participation can't find anyone who wants to come in and do an equity participation on this house. If we have everybody taking Barney's lecture on equity participation in a particular city, then after awhile all the real estate agents in Kansas City will understand what Barney is talking about when he runs an equity participation ad. Therefore, they will be able to bring their people over to my people and vice versa and we could do a lot more deals. That's one of the reasons I like to teach. But until you get a broad market, you keep missing each other.

Advertisements That Work

Try running this one: PAYMENTS LESS THAN BUYING PLUS THE BENEFITS OF OWNERSHIP. See how much the phone rings.

IF YOU'LL PAY A LITTLE MORE THAN RENT WE'LL GIVE YOU HALF THE HOUSE. Run an ad like that and see how many people start calling in.

The one I like is RICH UNCLE WILLING TO PUT DOWN PAYMENT UP FOR DESERVING YOUNG COUPLE, call such and such. You'll get lots of calls on that one.

Mom Buys Half Son Buys Half

Let me give you some ideas on the 3A situation. When are some other times when 3A makes sense, a new buyer and a tenant/buyer?

"Mom, you've been so good to me. You've raised me right. You taught me all the good things in life. It's just been so fantastic being your child. Will you buy me a new house?" You can imagine that kind of conversation taking place.

"Yes. You're a good kid and thanks for the compliments but you're the oldest of three. There are others coming behind you. Besides that Dad and I need a little bit of tax shelter ourselves. We're not going to go out and buy you houses. If anybody is going to buy anybody houses, we're going to buy us houses!"

"Mom, what I need is just a simple $20,000 check in a gift letter that says this is a gift so that I can go down and show the Savings and Loan so I can qualify for the loan because it has to be a gift."

"You're crazy. We're not going to do that!"

"Don't you want to help me out?"

"Okay, tell you what we'll do. We'll buy the house and put the money up. You move in and make all the payments at current financing rates. You'll own half and we'll own half. We'll get the tax shelter that we need now and several years from now when you decide to move and sell the property, we'll get some of our money back for retirement, You'll have a little bit of a nestegg to go out and buy your own house then."

Four More Combinations

The senior partner has some money to put down and doesn't want to mess with the house. The junior partner says he will come in and play the role of a #3. He'll just rent the house and take it over just like he's a #3. He'll cover the negative cash flow and then turn around and sublease it to a #1.

So we have A/3/1.

You, senior partner, put the money down on a house I buy and you get half the benefits and a very passive situation. I'll rent the doggone thing at a break even and cover the payments and all that and I'll get half so it gives me some tax shelter for nothing down. Then, I'll turn around and lease it for as high a price as I can lease it for and manage it so you're in a totally passive position. What am I doing? I end up making myself the cash flow investor by combining myself as a 3 with a 1. I end up being a C, covering the negative cash flow that's in there. That's wrapping around and becoming AN INVESTOR/INVESTOR AGREEMENT AGAIN.

There are dozens and dozens of combinations on this that make sense. You could have this combination. A 3, a C, and a A or B. A 3/C/A or a 3/C/B. I don't like this format but I've got to tell you about it because it exists.

This has been done on the west coast. They say they will bring two investors in. One of them will put the down-payment up and one of them will cover the negative cash flow and another one will pay part of the negative cash for a part interest in the property. They make it a 3-way split of the property.

Another approach used is this: I'm the equity investor. I'll pay half the down payment. You, the tenant/buyer (3), will pay half the down payment. On a monthly basis you will only pay an amount equal to rent and I will cover the negative cash flow difference. I can see some virtues to this in that the guy that moved in now has some money at stake. It is rather complicated from a tax point of view. Letter rulings have been made on some of these other forms but I don't think there has been a letter ruling on this one. You can see all the ways you can jockey this around if you wanted to design it to fit your own personal circumstances.

Chapter Fifteen

I suppose we could have a tenant/buyer who would say - I'll tell you what, I'll pay the down payment. I've got that. It's those monthly payments I can't afford. I need a C. I'll put the down payment down. You cover the negative cash flow and I'm going to have you cover a big chunk of it for me, and I'll give you half interest. I've got a house I can buy for 5% down. You cover the negative cash flow and I'll give you half interest for doing that. I'll bring in an investor who will be the passive investor who will cover the negative cash flow.

Think About This One

Here's a fun one I call a 0/A/C. Let me explain how it works. "A" is a new buyer. "C" is a cash flow investor. Now I don't have a patent on this. I've done a lot of the investor/investor agreements and the lease with option to buy, and I am putting together the tenant/buyer programs now. I'll have some of those closed real soon.

But what about this idea? Theoretically it is possible. Let's say you have a $64,000 first, a $16,000 equity, on an $80,000 house. You're living in this house. You find an investor. You say, Mr. Investor if you pay half the down payment ($8,000) and cover the negative cash flow, which would be $300 per month, let's say, I'll give you half the house. He just might say yes.

The problem is, when you run this ad, two people apply to do the deal, so you take both of them! One of them gives you $8,000 for half interest and the other one gives you $8,000 for half interest. One of them gives you $300 a month to cover the negative cash flow and the other one gives you $300 a month to cover the negative cash flow. If the payments on the house are actually $900 per month, you live in a house for rent of -$300 per month and you've pooled all your cash back out again to go out and reinvest. I have never done this and have never worked it out, but in theory it works. It's something to think about.

You Live Rent Free

Let's say you have this $80,000 house and you go to somebody and say, "How would you like to get in on a good deal?" Have I got a deal for you today! For nothing down I'll sell you half interest in this house. All you do is cover the negative cash flow, nothing down, $450 per month. You get two investors like that and you have both investors paying $450 per month. The payment on the house is $900 per month and YOU LIVE IN THERE FOR FREE. Now you do have your $16,000 equity in there which you don't get back until they decide to sell. Maybe your "cost" of living in the house is the fact that you're not getting a cash flow on that $16,000 equity. But, folks, if you bought the house for nothing down, $16,000 below appraised value, what you have is $16,000 that will be paid to you in the future and you live for free and have $16,000 whenever the house gets sold. Again, we're talking theory, but wouldn't it be fun?

Personally, I am working on the numbers for a $250,000 home to see how that works out, because I happen to know a rather large fellow who owns one and would like to live free... leaving his mythical equity tied up in it!

Equity Sharing Option

In talking about all the variations couldn't we also put together a limited partnership to take out all the cash flow investors? There are a dozen variations on this. Couldn't the equity investor (Mr. B) the owner/developer, do 100 houses with equity participation with $20,000 equity in each. He could then list with an exchange broker and trade out that passive equity investment for some other kind of property he could move. Aren't all these possibilities there? Lot of flexibility here.

H.E.L.P.

HOMEOWNER'S EQUITY LEASE PARTICIPATION

What's the **H.E.L.P.** program? Very simply this. You have this house with a 20% down payment, and the payments are still $1,200 per month. It will only rent for $700 per month. You say, "Sir (Maam), pay me an extra $500 per month and I'll give you an option to buy—an option good for one year. They say they are not interested. Then you say," Okay, how about this? I'll give you an option to buy the property and the option is good for as long as you live there. It won't expire for, we could put an expiration date on it, maybe 10 years, 15 years, whatever you want. I'm easy. What do you have in mind?

They say, "Gee. I like that. But $500 a month? What's the option price?"

That's the kicker isn't it?

1. I'll tell you what. I will participate with you in the future price increases.

2. I'll participate with you in the equity buildup.

3. I'll participate with you in inflation, however you want to describe it.

4. You'll buy the house and half of the price will be what it will cost you today and the other half of the price will be what it will cost you tomorrow.

Let's say this is a $100,000 house and when you fund on the option it is worth $200,000.

We'll figure the price this way. Half of the house will be half of what it would have cost you today. Today, it is $100,000 house. So that means half the house will cost you $50,000. Half of the house in the future, if it is worth $200,000 would cost you $100,000. So you pay $150,000 at time of close for a $200,000 house. You pick up $50,000 in benefits.

Chapter Fifteen

OPTION PRICE

Today's Price	Tomorrow's Price
$100,000	$200,000
$100,000 / 2 = $50,000	$200,000 / 2 = $100,000

$ 50,000

$100,000

$150,000 Purchase Price

YOUR "BONUS" AT SALE: $50,000!

We probably wouldn't run the agreement for 15 years. Odds are we would want to put a stop to it after maybe 7-10 years. We don't want to get out there too far. Maybe 5 years. Whatever you are comfortable with. I am not going to set rules for you. I am going to give you guidelines. You can figure what makes sense for your own marketplace and for the price of property you are working with.

If I am buying *rental* houses, I would rather buy cheap rental houses. I would rather buy just below the medium price range for a neighborhood, or for a city. If I'm doing lease with option to buy I can afford to go into the more expensive house because I am attracting the home-owner type.

In this world there are two types of people. There are the users, acquirers, and estate builders with this form of equity participation. The users use, throw away, or walk away. And, you don't want a user for a program like this. You want somebody who wants to be an acquirer, an estate builder, and owner of property. Due to circumstances, they don't have the money for a down payment or they can't afford the heavy payments for a nothing down transaction, conventionally financed.

So, after you make your offer, they say, "Gee, I'm paying you $500 a month extra and now I get the right to buy this house. Half the price today and half the price in the future?"

You say, "That's right." By the way you can make it one-third, two-thirds, or two-thirds, one-third, whatever makes you happy. You see the idea is you are sharing the future appreciation, regardless of the split.

WHAT IF HE DOESN'T BUY?

Your professional buyer says, "I like that. But there's one big problem. What if I stay here for three years, pay you for three years and then I move out? I could have been putting that $500 a month in a savings account. Let's say I stay for 30 months. That adds up to a lot of money. That's $15,000 I've given you!"

With my program, we say that's no problem. *We'll give it back to you as long as you have stayed in the house at least 18 months*!

How do you give it back? There are several options available and you decide before you tell them. I don't know which you will like the best. Let me tell you some I have thought of.

1. You say, "We are going to have to sell this house if you move out. Therefore, we will give you your money back in one year or when the house sells, whichever comes first."

2. Or, you could say, "We'll give you half the money back in cash now and the rest we'll pay back at $500 a month until you are paid back." Now you have taken all the sting out of the program.

"We'll also give you credit for part of your rent paid, to go towards the purchase."

"How much? Not $500 per month."

"We'll give you credit for $600 per month towards the purchase price of the house?"

WITH A PACKAGE LIKE THAT YOU ARE GOING TO BE ABLE TO INDUCE PEOPLE INTO JOINING YOU IN THE HELP PROGRAM.

If they buy, $600 per month of their payment is credited toward purchase. If they don't buy - (and they move out in the way you described, which is to give a 90 day notice of intent to move) - they want their money back, and they have been on time during the entire period, they get their money back.

Owner Benefits

What about the other side? Are there enough benefits for you? You have to decide that. Let's look at it this way.

1. Can you afford to hold the house with a $500 a month negative cash flow? "I don't know." If you can afford one, can you afford two? If you can afford two, can you afford three?

   Otherwise, if you have a negative cash flow, there is a limit to the amount of money you can pay per month, therefore limiting the amount of properties you can afford to own.

   If you could get *your tenants to move in and cover all the negative cash flow*, there is theoretically no limit to the number of properties that you can buy.

2. The real genius of this idea from the owner's point of view, is this. If the tenant has an option to buy, you get *100% of the depreciation* and that's where it's really at. Using the H.E.L.P. format, you are investing in real estate with no negative cash flow and you get all of the depreciation, be-

cause you are the owner. They are the tenant with an option to buy. Until they fund on that option, they are still a tenant.

3. Another plus for the owner/investor. By setting up this program you have no negative cash flow and if they move out, you give them back their money—but you don't give them any interest on their money. *Folks, that's like having an interest free loan to cover your negative cash flow.* In fact, the thing you like most about the program is the guy that stays for five years and moves out. Odds are that's what's going to happen.

In the old lease with option programs that people used to put together, 9 out of 10 people never funded on their lease with option. That's usually due to the fact that most people can't get their down payment together and they can't qualify for loans and so on. That will probably hold true here. You are giving them a lot of credits but just because they have the right to buy the property doesn't mean that they are ever going to get their act together and go ahead and buy it. I found this out. I think you'll find 8 out of 10 will walk away with this program. Because one of Zick's laws that I discovered early, early in my investment career - If you ever give an investor the right to get all his money back and walk away at some point in time in his life he is going to ask for it. That's almost a rule.

With the **H.E.L.P.** program, if you give the tenant the right to walk away with a 90-day notice and you give him the money back within a year's time, sure enough he is going to ask for it at some time or other.

What about the fact that you give him credit for $600 per month toward the purchase price? He is already paying you $500 per month more than you would have gotten with the lease. All you're giving is $100 per month. He is giving you this money toward purchase, early in the game. Yes, you are giving him credit, but he gave you the money. So all you are really walking away from is $100 per month, not $600.

4. There's also *a time value to money*. I'd love to have somebody buy a house from me five years from now and start paying me today. I'd love to have him pay me $500 a month today to buy a house five years from now. There's a very, very heavy time value to money with interest rates as they are today.

5. So what about the fact that you're giving back the $100 per month. Did you notice the commission in there anywhere? No. *This doesn't involve a commission.* When you sell you usually have to have a real estate broker help you with the transaction. Or, you have to spend an awful lot of your own time in getting the job done. This way you get a telephone call - "Hey, the check's in the mail. I'm buying my property that I've been living in." Let's say it's been 30 months and you're out the $100 per month and that's a grand total of $3,000. The property has gone up to $150,000 and people would normally

Chapter Fifteen

charge a $10,000 commission. You've lost $3,000 but you would have paid a $10,000 commission. How much have you lost?

6. Also, when you sell a house after a tenant moves out what do you usually have to do. 1. You have to go in and *clean it up*. 2. You have to fix a lot of things and *make a lot of repairs*. 3. That means you sit with *the house off the market for a month* or so while you do the fix up and then you usually have to *wait a month or two to sell it*. You are sitting there with no income coming in and a lot of income going out. So you don't have any loss, by adding the $100 as an incentive to stay.

BALANCING THE PLUSES AND MINUSES

What about the fact that you are giving him half the future appreciation? Not much argument there. Gee, that's terrible. But looking at the rest of the benefits maybe it's worth it. Maybe it makes sense. Maybe you'll be happy.

If it does not appreciate, then, month by month you have received the tax benefits, have had all the cash flow necessary to cover the negative cash flow, and then you have to repay your loan, with no interest. I'll tell you, some of you are going out and borrowing the money, month by month, and paying interest on it. If property doesn't appreciate, you are going to be in a lot more trouble than I am, when I have to pay it back, with no interest!

If the owner under a **H.E.L.P.** program was really smart, he would say that he wants to exercise his option and then go and stick a sign in the yard and sell it to somebody else and cash out. Somehow they just don't ever do that.

The one thing we forgot to talk about is how do they pay you when they buy. CASH. All cash. Which means somebody has to go out and get a new loan.

Are we taking advantage of the poor guy moving in? No. The person who sincerely wants to buy the house and doesn't have the down payment today but can afford to make those kind of monthly payments wants to have an offset that tells him that if things go wrong, he gets his money back. You know, if he bought the house contract for deed he wouldn't get the money back. What's he giving away for the right to get his money back. Depreciation. That's okay. I'll do that trade off with him. I personally feel that it is a very well balanced program with benefits between the owner and the potential owner.

You don't get depreciation when you are living in there because you are a tenant but you would get to *write off the taxes and the interest* and a lot of them don't realize the power of that kind of deduction.

If I were the person out there I would prefer to buy under one of the other programs of equity sharing where I get a deed to half interest. As a seller it really bothers me giving a deed to a tenant. The reason is, tenants are generally users and they are consumers. I've never met a tenant that I knew for sure I liked! I hold everything in judgment until they move out because I don't know if I've been done dirty until then!

The motivating factors for people to get involved in this **H.E.L.P.** form of equity participation that involves tenants are many. But just consider these points.

1. How do I get my negative cash flow covered if I don't get involved?

2. The person who has a share of future profits, or feels he has a share of future profits, will theoretically take much better care of the property, than one who is just a user.

3. How many of you like to go out on a Saturday afternoon to show properties? One of the nicest things about involving a tenant in a program like this is you are likely to get a tenant who will stay there much longer. You will have much less vacancy, much less fix up, and you won't have to go out and show the property all the time. These are some tremendous advantages.

I have tried to make the **H.E.L.P.** package as appealing to the person moving in as I can and still have it make economic sense for me.

Every property will be different because every property will have a different interest rate on the loan. If you are paying a huge interest rate on the loans on the property and you are not in that high of a tax bracket you may not be able to give away half the future appreciation. You may not be able to give away that much credit per month toward purchase. You are going to have to run your own numbers. I'm giving you a kind of model format to go after.

One of the other benefits here is - *who keeps the deed? I do*. There's a lot of power in having an option. Options aren't something to mess around with. You have to make sure they are drawn properly and when people move out you have to get a Quit Claim Deed or a release of some kind. You have to go through a lot of procedures. But an option still has a lot less power than a deed. I would rather have the deed in my name. That's one of the things that bothers me about some of the other forms of equity participation.

If this makes sense when you are paying loans with high interest rates, think what will happen if you have property in a positive position. It's going to be fantastic, because you talk about a positive cash flow. You have this property with a break even because you have a low interest rate, low balance loan on it. *All of a sudden you have a $500 a month positive cash flow out of a rental house*. What are you giving away? Future appreciation.

I think if I were 65 and concerned about my retirement I would love to enter into a 5-year **H.E.L.P.** program with somebody. All of a sudden this rental house of mine which I was thinking I would have to sell or refinance, is kicking me out $500 per month. If I had 10 of them I would have a lot of friends!

Chapter Fifteen

Equity Sharing Option

I think if I were 65 and concerned about my retirement I would love to enter into a 5-year H.E.L.P. program with somebody. All of a sudden this rental house of mine which I was thinking I would have to sell or refinance, is kicking me out $500 per month. If I had 10 of them I would have a lot of friends!

What about the guy who's going to come into your nice house on this plan, but really is going to tear it up and move away just like everybody else? How many people want to move away from a $15,000 security deposit? Not very many. *I love having a $15,000 security deposit*!

Now, it's true you only start out with a $500 security deposit the first night. You can put however many months you want into your agreement. I've said in my agreement that thou shalt not ask for any of your money back until you have been in there at least 18 months. So, I know I have at least an 18-month lease because they have $9,000 sitting there at that point in time. I'm willing to look at a good deal with them. Sure, they are going to have $9,000 more paid into the property before they have the right to get any money back.

I think there may be a chance somebody could take you to court and argue that it is unreasonable for you to keep all of that money. I don't know whether they would or not. I don't think they would win every time. But, I know if you write this up as a lease and you give credit for so much to be applied to the option, then monthly payments are lease payments. They would have a hard time asking for lease payments back for property they leased. The courts might let them have some of their money back but I guarantee they wouldn't let them have the money back for the damage they did to your house.

Do you know that as you receive option money it is not taxed to you until the option expires or is exercised. I am getting $1,200 per month and I'm willing to give a credit of $600 per month towards purchase. Isn't that $600 a month option money or at least $500 of it is option money because that is in excess of what you would have charged for rent? So I am receiving between $500-$600 worth of money without paying any taxes on it now. *Then when I do sell later on it's going to be capital gains*. That's going to appeal to somebody in a high tax bracket.

You get 100% of the depreciation, plus the money you're getting to cover payments and the negative cash flow and you're not paying any taxes on it.

Suppose you're 60 years old, working for a major corporation, have a heavy, heavy, taxable income, and you're planning to retire at age 65. You have this house sitting there, and all of a sudden you have this $500 a month positive cash flow coming in —with no taxes to pay on the $500 a month positive cash flow, plus full depreciation on the whole house.

I just think it hums!

Chapter Fifteen

Chapter Fifteen

Chapter Sixteen

Estate Building With Down Payment Partners

Matching Needs

Many exciting and potentially exciting real estate transactions require a great deal of money for the down payment. Borrowing that money increases your risk and your debt load. Rather than borrowing the down payment, (assuming you don't have the money yourself), the benefits of real estate ownership still can be yours if you're willing to share them with a down payment partner.

Wealthier people, (the ones who have $30,000 to $300,000 dollars to use as a down payment), usually don't have the time to seek out real estate investment opportunities. Even though the investor with $30,000 to invest might have more time than the person with $300,000, there are fewer small deals available, (ones that really make good sense), than there are large transactions. So, no matter <u>how much</u> money your client has to invest, he doesn't have a great deal of time, he needs your help.

You'll be paid for your time, negotiating skill and management expertise—as well as rewarded for good luck. It takes time to find good deals. It takes time to find any deal. If you spend that time and find reasonable, workable deals, you will locate a partner just because the transaction makes sense and he doesn't have the time. Through good negotiations (or sheer luck) you'll get a superior deal, get paid more and you can find a partner faster. The same holds true for management. The higher your level of experience, the faster people will sign up. However, if you're a hard worker and will diligently oversee management performed by other professionals, that alone will be enough to put some deals together in the first place.

Working With Others

Quite often I obtain options that are available because I'm involved with the management of the property. I work with a lot of passive investors, people who have money and no time. They desperately want a hedge against inflation and they really want to get invested. Since they don't want management responsibilities and many don't want to hire management, they need a partner or similar contractual agreement.

The format will vary depending on the client's needs and especially on the type of transaction. HERE'S MY FAVORITE.

I will have the option to buy a one-half undivided interest for one dollar after the return of their invested capital. This means if you put $20,000 down, when we sell the property they get the first $20,000 out and then we split the profit above that. That makes my investor a passive investor.

I take care of all the work. I take care of all the management. In all states I know of property management requires a real estate license--check on your local requirements if you want a license. However, no license is needed if you own or are renting the property, as under a lease option.

Sometimes I'm also paid a small management fee and sometimes I'm not, depending on the circumstances of the particular transaction. Most often I only receive a share of the profits. The day to day management is done by an outside firm and the expenses are be paid by the investor. But these usually don't amount to much, depending on how management intensive it is.

By owning the property in his own name, the investor will receive

100% of the depreciation. I get paid 50% of the future profits for finding the deal, putting it together, and taking care of it from then on out. In some situations I've even agreed to make a loan to

them should the property ever go into a negative cash flow and I'm not going to do that unless I'm very, very sure.

Fifty percent would be a lot to pay for just management. But as you can see, I do much more than just that. Often the deal is one where a lot of work needs to be done, especially solving old tenant or vacancy problems. This means both opportunity and potential profits, but more work and more expertise is needed than the investor can or wants to contribute.

There are lots of people who will manage your property for a fee of 6% of gross rents. The fee on single family houses is usually 10% or more and I don't want to do it for a 10% fee, let alone 6%. It's not worth doing unless your goal is to have a large property management company. And what day-to-day manager wants to wade into a nest of problems? However, I will do it for a percentage of the future profits. That way the passive investor gets all the depreciation. I just get a portion of the appreciation.

Chapter Sixteen

Estate Building With Down Payment Partners

The Down Payment Partner concept was developed by a student of mine, Donna Leadbetter, who bought over $4 million in property over a three-year period of time, using Down payment Partners.

She received national attention, appearing on many television shows because of her phenomenal success as a real estate investor, she made the cover of Money Magazine in 1985 and was asked to lecture around the country on the subject. Together we authored a course on the subject.

Because her transactions were all in the state of Florida, not everybody will be able to use the exact documentation she used. The agreements included herein are presented as a guideline only, a shortcut for your own custom-drawn document. You should pick the approach you want to use, then have a local real estate attorney help you customize your documents. However for illustrative purposes, there's nothing better than looking at someone else's successful system.

Choosing the right attorney is one of the most important steps for you to consider.

Documenting Your Deal

The documentation is probably the most important aspect of joint ownership or common investing in property. Even if you have the best standard documentation in the world drawn up by real estate experts, you will always improve your situation by going to a competent real estate lawyer. Now let me be more specific.

I personally think you would be better off taking a standard document that is well drawn and, without seeing an attorney, use it for the purpose it was designed. This would be better than drawing up your own documentation or modifying a standard document by yourself or going to see an attorney who isn't an expert in real estate.

You would be safe trusting a good real estate attorney without providing him with standard documentation to work from, but you take the chance of paying high legal fees.

How do you know when you're working with good real estate attorneys? I can promise that asking them directly, won't do the job. Not everybody has a copy of Martindale Hubbel, the book in which all lawyers list their names and reveal their specialties.

Ask your local title company, escrow firm or a couple of real estate brokers who they would use. When I say ask brokers, I don't mean sales representatives, I mean the person who owns the company. They can tell you what lawyer handles their real estate business and that should be a good clue.

If you want to interview an attorney to find out if he or she is a good prospect as your real estate attorney, here are some questions:

Chapter Sixteen

1. "What are your specialties — the areas in which you have the most experience and in-depth knowledge?" By asking the question in this way, you are not asking whether they are a real estate attorneys, which would get you a quick yes. Listen to the answer carefully to see how real estate weighs in their dealings.

2. "Have you ever been involved in successfully drafting documents and closing a tax deferred exchange?" The reason you ask this question is because exchanges are probably one of the most sophisticated real estate transactions anyone can try to accomplish. If this attorney can successfully complete an exchange, he or she is probably a good candidate for handling your affairs. The more exchanges they has done, the better.

3. "Have you ever put together a real estate syndication? Was this syndication registered with the state and was it registered with the federal government?" Syndications are a special area of law. You have to have syndication knowledge as well as real estate knowledge. When it comes to drafting unusual real estate contracts like the ones we are discussing, a good part of the solution is the ability to draft contracts and to understand relationships of parties within a transaction, when those parties have different roles to play.

One of the best attorneys I ever worked with on real estate transactions is not as much of a real estate expert as he is a joint venture, small and large syndication pro. He has handled ma and pa stores to SEC registrations of companies that ended up going on the stock exchange. He owns and invests in real estate and has done some real estate syndications. His real estate knowledge combined with superior syndication skills make him a good lawyer for me.

4. "How many years have you practiced law and in what field did you get your undergraduate degree?" Unfortunately, they don't tell you how to practice law in law school. Law school teaches what the laws are and how they work. You don't learn about the business world or financial relationships or money until you have been out there dealing with it yourself.

Somewhere in the third or fourth year of practice you get to where you know what you are doing. You'll know what you are doing quicker if you have an undergraduate degree in accounting or business administration or at least economics. If you got your degree in underwater basket weaving or even in English, you may never know what you are doing when it comes to business.

One of the sharpest attorneys I ever worked with on negotiating and contract drafting of good old fashioned real estate deals has his undergraduate degree in accounting. He can just about figure your mortgage in his head and he can give you an idea of your tax savings without getting out a pencil.

A good way to control your legal costs is to set up a maximum fee from the beginning. I GUESS WHAT I AM SAYING IS THAT A GOOD ATTORNEY

IS WORTH HIS WEIGHT IN GOLD and the more you plan to do deals like this, the more important it becomes for you to get someone who knows what he or she is doing.

5. The best question, if you have the gall, is "How much real estate do you currently own?" **I'd never trust a naked tailor.** Nor would I trust a real estate attorney who lived in an apartment, unless he owned the building!

Donna's Documents

Donna had a special advantage, being from the State of Florida where they use land trusts. Only a handful of states have officially recognized the use of the land trust. The land trust is like a bucket in which you can carry your title. It stands on its own and the title to the real estate is carried in this entity or bucket. You can pass along the right to the beneficial interest in the trust, (the right to carry a bucket), to another person without ever having to re-record the deed.

If the trust is shown as the owner of a piece of property, you don't have to sell the property, you just have to change beneficiaries of the trust.

Second, Donna basically used the "option to purchase a one half- interest to buy the property" concept.

Somebody else puts up the money to buy the property. You, the investor who found the property, get an option to buy one half the equity in the property for one half of what your investor paid.

Thus, if your investor put up $50,000 to buy the property, you can buy half the equity back for $25,000. This way you're locked into half the future appreciation.

Also, since the investor has the property titled in his name, he gets 100% of the tax benefits. After the 1986 Tax Reform Act, this might be one of the few "tax smart" ways left for a money partner to still qualify for tax write-offs!

In the next section of this text, we're going to show you the types of documents Donna would use to do her transactions in your state. We will later show you the exact forms she used in the State of Florida, but since those forms are not universally applicable to all 50 states, in the first set we've "translated" them into forms that should be usable in all 50 states We did not include a copy of the deed you would use; but provided the words to put on the deed. Each state has their own deed forms.

The special documents you'll need, such as the notice of option, are enclosed, as are other document references.

Document Checklist

1. INITIAL PURCHASE CONTRACT—You need to "tie down" the subject property. You can do this by signing a purchase contract. If you do, try to make sure you can back out of the contract but the seller can't.

Chapter Sixteen

Possible clause "This contract is subject to the approval of my financing partner. Said approval to be provided seller in writing no later than five days prior to closing."

Or, you can use an option to purchase. If you use an option, you can purchase a standard form from any business stationary store. That's also the place to get a real estate contract that's valid in your state.

2. CONTRACT WITH DOWN PAYMENT PARTNER—There are several approaches to signing up your "Down Payment Partner" or money partners. Here are the two easiest:

    A. Use a real estate sales contract. You can sign a contract from you to your money partner, even though you don't yet own the property. All you have to do is to be able to deliver the property, which you can, by way of your purchase contract or option.

    B. Use an assignment of contract. You can include reference to all the arrangements that you and your investor have agreed to with an assignment like the one that follows. This is best because it avoids the IRS claiming it was a sale-lease-back between you and the money partner.

In either event, you close both your initial purchase with the seller directly to the money partner. Thus, you don't have to come up with anything but escrow money.

Remember to get your option money or escrow money back at the close. If you assign the contract, the amount paid in cash for the contract should, at a minimum, reimburse all your out-of-pocket costs. Charge any more than that, and you'll walk away with a cash profit.

3. PROPERTY MANAGEMENT OR LEASE BACK AGREEMENT—Donna's approach was to include property management and to charge a fee for it. Of course, Donna had a real estate license, which is required in most states if you charge for property management.

I've used that approach, but here's a good variation. You hire a property manager but you are responsible for supervising him. This way you don't need a license. Also, you can hire someone to do less than all the work because of your participation. (For instance, you don't need a real estate license to do accounting.) This "active" or "passive" investor category is an important part of the 1986 tax legislation.

Often, I'll lease the property. A proper lease is better for the money partner than a management contract. Read the "Lease Option" section of this Hidden Profits text.

If you are going to pay all costs, then make the property break even so that the rent charged will be enough "to pay all taxes, insurance, principal and interest and normal maintenance".

In general, it's better to close using an assignment of contract, especially if you're planning to lease back the property. The negative tax implications if you bought (actually went into title) and then sold and then leased back are a loss of write offs for your money investor. The IRS currently refers to sale-lease-backs as "financing arrangements". They treat the property owner as if he were a lender. If you only plan to property manage, it doesn't make much difference tax-wise. However, if the money partner ends up buying directly (because you assign the contract to him and he closes) you have fewer problems later on.

4. DEED WITH NOTICE OF OPTION—I protect myself by placing a short notice about my option on the face of the deed. It also could be a separate document. The notice would be very short and placed on the face of the deed where all liens are listed. It would read as follows:

"This property is subject to an option to purchase with Bernard Zick, PO Box 630, Solana Beach, CA 92075. Anyone dealing in or with the subject property should contact Zick for specific terms of the option."

Donna had an option to purchase the "beneficial interest" in the land trust. That wouldn't be relevant to 90% of our readers. Thus we present a notice of option to purchase, with the notice placed on the deed and one done separately.

5. OPTION—The last agreement is the option that allows you to buy half the equity for half what the money partner has in it.

(About the "Notary"... All states allow a person to become licensed as a notary. A notary can officially witness a signature which also is required if the document is to be recorded. Some states are very picky as to what format should be used. Most business supply houses have pads of notary forms or contact your local county recorder's office to get what's approved.)

ASSIGNMENT OF CONTRACT

I, _____, the undersigned, do hereby assign transfer and convey unto _____, investor, all my rights, title and interest in that certain Real Estate Contract dated _____ day of _____, 19___ between _____(seller) and the undersigned as buyer, for property legally described as:

(LEGAL DESCRIPTION)

Chapter Sixteen

with a copy of the contract being attached and by this reference being made a part hereof, for the sum of $_____, paid to the undersigned by investor, and with further consideration of a lease with option to buy (or management contract with option to buy) agreement being signed by the undersigned and the investor relating to the subject property.

_____

(NAME)   (DATE)

_____   (NAME)

(DATE)

STATE OF _____

COUNTY OF _____

ATTACH NOTARY HERE

NOTICE OF OPTION AGREEMENT

NOTICE, all people dealing in and with the following legally described property are hereby notified that the owners of said property, Ann Carole, a divorced woman, have, for consideration received, entered into an option agreement dated in November, 1986, with Bernard Zick and said option having a term of ten years, and containing a prohibition against borrowing subsequent to the date of granting the option. The property is legally described as follows:

(Legal)

All parties dealing in or with the subject legally described property should contact Bernard Zick, PO Box 630, Solana Beach, CA 92075, for the particulars which are included in the option agreement.

_____ June 16, 1986

Ann Carole

STATE OF _____)

COUNTY OF _____)

On this _____ day of _____, before me, a Notary Public, personally appeared _____ and _____ who

Chapter Sixteen

executed the above and foregoing instrument and acknowledged that they executed the same as their free act and deed.

IN WITNESS WHEREOF, I have hereunto set my hand and affixed my seal the day and year first above written.

_____ PUBLIC NOTARY My Commission Expires _____

NOTICE OF OPTION AGREEMENT

NOTICE, all people dealing in and with the following legally described property are hereby notified that the owners of said property, _____ _____ has for consideration received, entered into an option agreement dated _____ with _____ and said option having a term of _____ and containing a prohibition against borrowing subsequent to the date of granting the option. The property is legally described as follows:

(Legal)

All parties dealing in or with the subject legally described

property should contact _____

for the particulars which are included in the option agreement.

Dated this _____ day of _____, 19____.

_____

(NAME)

STATE OF _____

COUNTY OF _____

ATTACH NOTARY HERE

THIS JOINT VENTURE AGREEMENT, made and executed this _____ day of _____, 19____, by and between _____, hereinafter called "Investor" and _____, hereinafter called "MGR", hereby and herewith create a Joint Venture between the parties hereto for the sole purpose of acquiring and selling that certain real estate more particularly described on Exhibit "A" hereto attached and made a part hereof, the same as if fully set out herein, all of said real estate hereinafter called "the Property".

In consideration of the mutual promises and covenants hereinafter contained, the parties hereto agree as follows:.

1. MGR shall immediately upon the execution of this Agreement initiate appropriate action necessary to acquire title or an option to acquire title to "the Property" but only for a price and only upon such terms and conditions as are hereafter agreed upon in writing by Investor and MGR. MGR agrees that he will make no contracts or agreements, either orally or in writing, with regard to the acquisition of any interest in "the Property" in behalf of this Joint Venture until the price for such acquisition and the terms and conditions thereof are agreed upon in writing by Investor and MGR.

2. Investor agrees that he will furnish all funds necessary to purchase "the Property" in accordance with any contract of purchase entered into by the parties hereto with the present owner or owners of "the Property". Title to "the Property", or the interest therein acquired by this Joint Venture, shall be taken in the names of Investor and MGR.

3. Immediately after the parties hereto have acquired title to "the Property", or such other interest as they may acquire, MGR agrees to use his best efforts to sell and dispose of the interest so acquired by the parties hereto; however, no sale or disposition of the interest of the parties hereto in "the Property" shall be made and no contracts or agreements, either orally or written, pertaining to the sale or disposition of "the Property", or any interest therein, shall be made by MGR until the parties hereto have in writing agreed upon the sales price and all other terms and conditions of such sale or disposal.

4. The parties hereto shall share equally in all of the profits realized from the acquisition and sale of "the Property" and, further, shall bear equally any losses which may be sustained in connection with such acquisition and sale, EXCEPT AND PROVIDED THAT MGR shall not be entitled to share in any profits, proceeds or revenues received by this Joint Venture from the sale or disposition of "the Property", or in any assets of this Joint Venture, until Investor shall have been reimbursed in cash or other assets acceptable to Investor in lieu of cash for all moneys advanced and paid by Investor for the purchase and acquisition of "the Property" or the Joint Venture's interest in "the Property" described in Exhibit "A" hereto attached. Investor shall be reimbursed for such moneys paid and advanced by him immediately after the first and subsequent sales or

dispositions of all or any part of "the Property" to the extent that cash funds or other assets acceptable to Investor in lieu of cash are available for such purposes from any such sale or disposition after payment of all necessary sales expenses of any such sale or disposition. Any real estate commissions to which either of the parties hereto may be entitled by reason of such sale or disposition shall not be deemed a "necessary sales expense" as that term is used in this paragraph. .

5. No obligations or liabilities shall be incurred by either of the parties hereto pertaining to the subject matter and the purpose of this Joint Venture without the written concurrence of the other party.

6. The rights and interests of the parties in this Agreement or the Joint Venture hereby created, nor any of the assets of this Joint Venture are assignable except by operation of law or the mutual consent of both of the parties hereto.

7. If not sooner terminated, the Joint Venture hereby created shall terminate upon death or incompetency of either of the parties hereto. Upon the death or incompetency of either party, the remaining party and the personal representative of the deceased or incompetent party shall immediately wind up the affairs of this Joint Venture, divide the assets and adjust and pay the profits and losses of this Joint Venture between the remaining party and the deceased or incompetent party's estate in accordance with the terms of this Agreement.

8. Unless sooner terminated as above provided or by the mutual agreement of the parties hereto, this Joint Venture shall terminate at such time as all of the interest which the parties hereto may acquire in "the Property" has been sold and disposed of by the parties in accordance with the terms and conditions of this Joint Venture. Upon the sale and disposal of "the Property", the affairs of this Joint Venture shall be wound up and all profits and losses adjusted and paid by the parties in accordance with the terms of this Joint Venture as above set forth.

IN WITNESS WHEREOF, the parties have hereunto set their hands and seals the day and year first above written.

_____

Investor_____

MGR_____

Calculating Tax Benefits

The maximum tax advantages accrue to your cash partner in the Down Payment Partner format. Since the money partner has 100% title to their property, they get 100% of the tax write-offs. Your option has no tax effects if you structure things properly.

Most of your tax savings will come from depreciation. For properties purchased on or after January 1st, 1987, the depreciation schedule is 27 1/2 years straight line <u>for residential properties</u>. Depreciation is figured as the purchase price less the value of the land, divided by 27 1/2. (The IRS requires you to use a reasonable value for the land, not an artificially low one. They will settle for the tax assessor's land-to-value ratio applied to the purchase price.) Thus, if the tax assessor valued the building at $60,000 and the land at $10,000 then the land to value ratio is 1 to 7. Divide your purchase price by 7, the result is the land value. Subtract that from the purchase price and the remainder (6/7ths) is the depreciable building value.

EXAMPLE:

$$\frac{700{,}000}{7} = 100{,}000 \text{ land}$$

$700,000 Cost
-100,000
600,000 Building.

The new tax law limits tax write-offs to $25,000. If cash-in is equal to cash-out, otherwise, if your cash operating expenses are equal to rents and miscellaneous income, then your only write-off is depreciation.

Unless the new tax law is revised, investors will want their properties to break even..at a minimum. (A positive cash flow is better!) This will require large down payments. **That's why the Down Payment Partners concept is still workable.**

Where else can an investor look for tax shelter? The limited partnership won't work. The investor needs to own at least 10% interest in the property. In most large syndications you'd have a 1/1000 interest with $50,000 invested. Here they get 100% ownership and 100% of the write-off.

I've worked it backwards.

$$\frac{\$687{,}570}{27.5} = \$25{,}002.55$$

Thus, one investor could have $687,000 in depreciable property and be allowed $25,000 in write-offs.

There are other limitations. There are three types of income: earned, passive and portfolio. Earned income is wages, commission etc. All real estate activities are said to be "passive". If your real estate activities as a group generate, losses, up to $25,000 of the losses, can be used to write- off against other income. That assumes:.

1. You own 10% or more of the property; and,

2. You "actively participate" in running it.

Chapter Sixteen

How do we satisfy the "actively participate" rule? The money partner doesn't want to do the work. That's fine. Congress said in committee that you could still actively participate <u>even if</u> you hire a property manager. Some evidence of active participation could include setting tenant screening policy, tenant rules, etc. Sounds to me like you, the working partner had best put all that in writing and get the money parties approval. I'd go so far as writing a letter to set a date to discuss property management items. Have that meeting and keep notes.

You may want to give the money partner the right to hire a professional property management company to replace you. As long as they hire a good one and you still get your share of the profits, that should be okay with you!.

Use the a Annual Property Operating Data (APOD) form to figure if the property will break even. This is the Realtor's name for a one year income statement for a property. Any such form will work. We've told you how to figure the depreciation.

There are other limits. The $25,000 write-off phases out above $100,000 in income. For each $1,000 of income over $100,000, you lose the use of $500 of depreciation. Thus, when your income is over $150,000 you can't use the tax shelter.

It would be most beneficial to have a good tax preparer or CPA help you project the tax consequences of your first deal or two. You assume a great liability if you get someone to invest based on expected tax savings and have the decision based on wrong numbers.

Calculating Tax

1. Calculate the individuals taxes without the tax saving investment.

2. Redo your taxes adding in the information about your investments — those that save you on taxes. The difference is you real dollar tax savings.

3. Look at the tax rate for the last dollar of income being taxed. The tax rate you will find is your "marginal tax bracket". This tells you that any new income will be taxed at this rate. Any savings will save you taxes at this rate. .

Most middle management people or self employed people at 28% and those who earn more are at 33%.

Too often people use all the wrong terms to describe tax savings. The terms above are the proper approaches to describing tax savings.

The first step is to be prepared. Have a "package" — an explanation as to what you are intending to do, information on the property, and something telling the investor what you expect him to do and what he will get for being involved.

Chapter Sixteen

Next, you have to get in front of investors that have enough money to do what you need to do. I am totally convinced that the following is true: THERE ARE MORE PEOPLE WITH MONEY THAN THERE ARE GOOD DEALS. If you can find a good deal, then you can eventually find the money.

Since time is always short, start lining up people that might make good investors NOW!.

Tell them what you have done and what you want to do. Speak in general terms and try to get them to see the benefits in doing a transaction with you.

Most everyone you write a check to is a possible investor. This includes the pet clinic, the auto dealer, the TV repair store owner, etc. .

Practice what you are going to say on a friend first. Do not get discouraged. Remember what they tell sales people.. if one out of ten people buy, then the first five "no's" just put you closer to the eventual "yes!".

Remember: 1) The more time you study the material, the better you'll be able to explain benefits to others. 2) Learn to figure tax benefits so you can show dollar and cents savings examples to investors. 3) Stay up to date on tax law changes. 4) Use a good attorney to do your documents. If you take good care of your money partners, some day the deals will start taking care of you!

OPTION AGREEMENT

This Agreement dated the _____ day of _____, 19____ by and between the undersigned as Beneficiaries and/or Optionees to become Beneficiaries under that certain Trust.

For and in consideration of the Optionee, Donna Leadbetter, acquiring, consulting, agreeing to manage and to fund deficit according to terms of this agreement, the Optionor herein grants to and/or assigns to Donna Leadbetter for no additional consideration the option as herein described.

Name of Trust:

Name of Trustee:.

Date of Trust:

Res of Trust:.

The following terms shall apply throughout this document:.

Beneficiary #1 - Optionor #1

Beneficiary #2 - Optionee #1.

TERM OF OPTION

Chapter Sixteen

Each option shall commence on the _____ for a period of ten years thereafter.

OPTIONEE:

Optionee as herein and further referred to shall mean the Optionee, the assigns of the Optionee or partial assigns of the Optionee, heirs, executors, administrators, personal representatives or successors.

EXERCISE OF OPTION:

The Optionee shall have the right to exercise the option after _____ _____, 19_____, but before _____ _____, 19___.

NOTICE OF EXERCISE:

The exercise must be in writing and delivered to the Trustee with a copy to the Optionor at the address specified above.

OPTION PRICE:

$10.00 and pro rata assumption of all the existing obligations pertaining to the property.

MANAGEMENT CONTRACT:

The Optionee shall manage the property according to a management contract and any amendments thereto. All amendments must be in writing and signed by all parties.

MANAGEMENT:

Optionee shall be the manager of the property and shall have the right to assign the management of the property, but will still have the obligations of manager and among those obligations shall be the duty to pay 50% of the deficit _____. This payment shall be made in adjustments to the capital account and must be paid at least quarterly.

PRIOR TO THE EXERCISE OF THE OPTION:

1. FIRST RIGHT OF REFUSAL.

The Optionee, together with any future sub-optionees as their interest may appear, shall have a FIRST RIGHT OF REFUSAL as herein described. In the event that they shall agree between them not to exercise the FIRST RIGHT OF REFUSAL in concert, they may agree that one Optionee may purchase the interest of the other Optionee and that surviving Optionee shall then have the right to enter into the contract executing the FIRST RIGHT OF REFUSAL.

In the event of the submission of any contract to purchase, exchange, lease or lease/option any asset of the Trust by an outside "3rd party" in an "arms-length" transaction, the parties agree that there shall exist a FIRST RIGHT OF REFUSAL. Said FIRST RIGHT OF REFUSAL shall be for the Optionee and/or sub-optionee(s) to purchase, exchange, lease or lease/option the Trust asset being proposed for sale, etc. at the same price and terms as stipulated in the proposed sale, etc. Said FIRST RIGHT OF REFUSAL must be exercised by a written contract or lease within five working days after presentation of the original contract to the Trust. Closing on that contract shall be on or before the closing date stipulated in the original contract, however, no sooner than sixty days from date of original contract. All contracts for the exercise of the FIRST RIGHT OF REFUSAL defaulting, or in the alternative, applied to the purchase price at closing if the holder of the FIRST RIGHT OF REFUSAL does in fact close on the second contract.

2. MANDATORY PURCHASE OF OPTION INTEREST BY BENEFICIARIES PRIOR TO EXERCISE OF THE OPTION:

It is acknowledged by the parties that the Beneficiaries may sell their beneficial interest in the Trust or direct the Trustee to sell the property owned by the Trust during the term of the Option to purchase beneficial interest. In the event of a sale of either the Beneficial Interest or the Trust Property prior to the Optionee's exercise of the Option, then the Beneficiary shall be obligated to purchase the Option Interest of the Optionee under the following terms and conditions:

The Optionee shall receive 50% of the "net" cash or equity in kind. "Net" being defined as the difference of the gross sales price after sales costs and the outstanding mortgages and obligations among which shall be included the _____ which is due to the Optionor. The Optionor warrants that the obligations and mortgages referred to herein shall be limited to the following:

First mortgage:

A collateral assignment of the Beneficial Interest of the Optionor given to the Optionee to secure and warrant the Optionor's performance to keep all mortgages, taxes and insurance current at all times and to cause the property to be managed without waste. This collateral assignment shall be property executed and included in the documents filed with the Trustee as part of Trust.

FROM AND AFTER THE DATE OF EXERCISE OF THE OPTION:

1. The new Beneficiary(ies) shall participate in the income   pro rata.

2. The new Beneficiary(ies) shall participate in the expenses and tax deductions pro rata including, but not limited to: principal, interest, taxes, insurance, maintenance and expenses related to the subject property.

3. Upon Disposition of Trust Property.

The Optionee shall receive 50% of the "net" cash or equity in kind. "Net" being defined as the difference of the gross sales price after sales costs and the outstanding mortgages and obligations among which shall be included the _____ which is due to the Optionor. The Optionor warrants that the obligations and mortgages referred to herein shall be limited to the following:.

A collateral assignment of the Beneficial Interest of the Optionor given to the Optionee to secure and warrant the Optionor's performance to keep all mortgages, taxes and insurance current at all times and to cause the property to be managed without waste and to refinance or payoff any balloon mortgages or other liens as they shall become due. This collateral assignment shall be properly executed and included in the documents filed with the Trustee as part of Trust.

WARRANTIES AND COLLATERAL:

During the term of this Option Agreement, Donna L. Leadbetter as Optionee has conveyed 100% of whatever she may have for acquiring, consulting, agreeing to manage and to fund deficit according to terms of this agreement to _____ as Optionor under this arrangement based upon the warranties made by _____ that he will keep all mortgages, taxes and insurance, etc. current at all times and refinance or payoff mortgages as due and pay 50% of all monies due when the property is vacant. To further secure the Optionee as to that the warranties of the Optionor shall actually take place, the Optionor agrees to make a collateral pledge of his beneficial interest in such a fashion as is acceptable to the Optionee. This collateral assignment shall be labeled Addendum 1 and be included as an attachment to this document.

Failure on part of the Optionee, her heirs, or assigns to pay any monies owed to the capital account within 45 days and 15 days written notice, will result in a default on the option under the same terms and conditions as those found in the assignment of the beneficial interest found in this document.

_____

_____

Witness

_____

_____

Witness: Donna L. Leadbetter, Optionee.

Chapter Sixteen

State of _____

County of _____.

I HEREBY CERTIFY that on this day, before me, an officer duly authorized in the State aforesaid and in the County aforesaid to take acknowledgments, personally appeared _____ to me known to be the person(s) described in and who executed the foregoing instrument and ____ acknowledged before me that ____ executed the same.

WITNESS my hand and official seal in the county and State last aforesaid this _____ day of _____, A.D. 19___.

_____

Notary Public.

My Commission Expires

WARRANTY DEED TO TRUSTEE

THE GRANTOR <u>MR. AND MRS. X</u>.

of the County of <u>Pinellas</u> and State of <u>Florida</u>, for and in consideration of the sum of <u>TEN and NO/100 ($10.00) DOLLARS</u>, and other good and valuable considerations in hand paid, conveys, grants, bargains, sells, aliens, remises, releases, confirms and warrants under provisions of <u>Section 689.071 Florida Statutes</u>, <u>UNTO DONNA E. LEADBETTER</u>.

ADDRESS: <u>10 B Street, Clearwater, FL 33516</u>.

as Trustee under the provisions of a trust agreement dated the <u>17th</u> day of <u>January</u>, <u>1983</u> known as Trustee Number <u>122</u> the following described real estate in the County of <u>Pinellas</u>, State of <u>Florida</u>, to wit:.

Lot B, Block <u>C</u>, <u>Willow Creek</u>, according to plat thereof as recorded in <u>Plat Book 3</u>, Page <u>1</u>, of the Public Records of <u>Pinellas County, Florida</u>.

Together with all the tenements, hereditaments and appurtenance thereto, belonging or in anywise appertaining.

TO HAVE AND TO HOLD the said premises in fee simple forever, with the appurtenances attached thereto upon the trusts and for the uses and purposes herein and in said trust agreement set forth.

Full power and authority granted to said trustee, with respect to the said premises or any part of it, and at any time or times, to subdivide said premises or any part thereof, to dedicate parks, streets, highways or alleys and to vacate any subdivision or part thereof, and to resubdivide said property as often as desired, to contract to sell, to grant options to purchase, to on any terms to convey either with or without consideration, to donate, to mortgage, pledge or otherwise encumber said property, or any part thereof, to lease said property or any part thereof, from time to time, in possession or reversion by leases to commence in present or in future, and upon any terms and for any period or period of time, not exceeding in the case of any single demise the term of 198 years, and to renew or extend leases upon any terms and for any period or periods to time and to amend, change or modify leases and the terms and provisions thereof at any time hereafter, to contact to make leases and to grant options to lease and options to renew leases and options to purchase the whole or any part of the reversion and to contact respecting the manner of fixing the amount of present or future rentals, to partition or to exchange said property, or any part thereof, for other real or personal property, to grant easements or charges of any kind, to release, convey or assign any right, title or interest in or about or easement appurtenant to said premises or any part thereof, and to deal with said property and every part thereof in all other ways and for such other considerations as it would be lawful for any person owning the same to deal with the same, whether similar to or different from the ways above specified, at any time or times hereafter.

In no case shall any party dealing with said trustee in relation to said premises, to whom said premises or any part thereof shall be conveyed, contracted to be sold, leased or mortgaged by said trustee, be obliged to see to the application of any purchase money, rent, or money borrowed or advanced on said premises, or be obliged to see that the terms of this trust have been complied with, or be obliged to inquire into necessity or expediency of any act of said trustee, or be obliged or privileged to inquire into any of the terms of said trust agreement; and every deed, mortgage, lease or other instrument executed by said trustee in relation to said estate shall be conclusive evidence in favor of every person relying upon or claiming under such conveyance, lease or other instrument, (a) that at any time of the delivery thereof the trust created by this indenture and by said trust agreement was in full force and effect, (b) that such conveyance or other instrument was executed in accordance with the trusts, conditions and limitations contained herein and in said trust agreement or in some amendment thereof and binding upon all beneficiaries thereunder and (c) that said trustee was duly authorized and empowered to execute and deliver every such deed, trust deed, lease, mortgage or other instrument.

The interest of each and every beneficiary hereunder and of all persons claiming under them or any of them shall be only in the earnings, avails and proceeds arising from the sale or other disposition of said real estate, and such interest is hereby declared to be personal property. No beneficiary hereunder shall have any title or interest legal or equitable, in or to said estate as such, but only an interest in the earnings, avails and proceeds thereof as aforesaid.

AND the grantor hereby covenants with said grantee that the grantor is lawfully seized of said land in fee simple; that the grantor has good right and lawful authority to sell and convey said land; that the grantor hereby fully warrants the title to said land and will defend the same against the lawful claims of all persons whomsoever; and that said land is free of all encumbrances, except taxes accruing subsequent to December 31, 1983.

IN WITNESS THEREOF, the said grantor has hereunto set hand and seal the day and year first above written.

Signed, sealed and delivered

in our presence:

STATE OF: FLORIDA

COUNTY OF: PINELLAS

I HEREBY CERTIFY that on this day, before me, an officer duly authorized in the State aforesaid and in the County aforesaid to take acknowledgments, personally appeared.

MR. & MRS. X

to me known to be the person(s) described in and who executed the foregoing instrument and they acknowledged before me that they executed the same.

WITNESS my hand and official seal in the County and State last aforesaid this 19th day of January A.D., 19XX.

_____

Notary Public

My Commission Expires:

This instrument prepared by:

Donna's Land Trust Document

Since Donna was in the State of Florida, she had the advantage of using the Florida Land Trust Laws. Such laws are in existence in several other states including Illinois, where it initially gained broad use, and Hawaii. The trust ends up holding title to the property in trust name and usually only the trustee's name is disclosed.

Several specialized documents are necessary to accomplish this, one of the most important of which is some sort of a land/trust agreement between the parties. That's our first document.

LAND TRUST AGREEMENT

THIS TRUST AGREEMENT, dated this _____ day of _____ 19___ and known as Trust Number _____, to certify that _____ is about to take title to real estate under the provisions of Section 689.071, Florida Statutes, in the State of Florida, commonly known as, _____ _____, legally known as:

and that when _____ has taken title thereto, or to any other property conveyed to _____ as Trustee hereunder, _____ will hold it and the proceeds, profits, and avails thereof, if any, which may come into _____ possession by direction of the beneficiary or beneficiaries or by specific terms hereof, in Trust, for the ultimate use and benefit of the following named persons according to their respective interest herein set out, and assigns to wit:.

IT IS UNDERSTOOD AND AGREED by and between the Trustee and any person or persons who have or may become entitled to any interest under this trust, that the interests of any beneficiary hereunder shall consist solely of a power of direction to deal with the title to said property and the right to receive or direct the disposition of the proceeds from rentals and from the mortgages, sales, or other disposition of said premises; such right in the avails of said property shall be deemed to be personal property and may be treated, assigned and transferred as such, that in the case of death of any beneficiary hereunder during the existence of this trust, his or her right and interest shall, except as herein otherwise provided, pass to his or her personal representative and not to is or her heirs at law; and that no beneficiary now has or shall hereafter at any time have, any right, title, or interest in or to any portion of real estate as such, either legal or equitable, but only an interest in the earnings, avails and proceeds as aforesaid; it being the intention of this instrument to vest the full legal and equitable title to said premises in the Trustee. The death of any beneficiary hereunder shall not terminate the trust or in any manner affect the powers of the binding on the Trustee until the original and a duplicate copy of the assignment, in such form as the Trustee may approve, is lodged with it and its acceptance indicated thereon.

1. Confidentiality of Trust.

It shall not be the duty of the purchaser of the trust property of any part thereof to see to the application of the purchase money paid therefore; nor shall anyone who may deal with the Trustee be privileged or required to inquire into the necessity or expediency of or as to the provisions of this instrument.

2. Recording of Trust.

This trust agreement shall not be recorded or filed in the county in which the trust property is situated or elsewhere, except as hereinafter provided, but the recording or filing of the same shall not be considered as notice of the rights of any person derogatory to the title or powers of the Trustee.

3. Direction of the Trust.

Chapter Sixteen

While the Trustee is the sole owner of the real estate held by it hereunder and so far as the public is concerned and has full power to deal with it, it is understood and agreed by the persons in interest hereunder and by any persons who may hereafter become interested, that the Trustee will deal with it only when authorized to do so in writing and that it will (unless otherwise directed by the beneficiaries) on the written direction of or on the written direction of all the beneficiaries hereunder at the time, make contracts or deeds for the sale of or otherwise deal with the said real estate or any part thereof; provided, however, that the Trustee shall not be required to enter into any personal obligation or liability in dealing with said trust property or to make itself liable for any damages, costs, expenses, fines or penalties, or to deal with the title so long as any money is due to it hereunder, and to the extent of any monies due to it hereunder, it shall have a lien on the property or the proceeds thereof. Otherwise, the Trustee shall not be required to inquire into the propriety or purpose of any such direction.

4. Management of the Property.

The Beneficiary or beneficiaries hereunder shall have and retain (except as otherwise expressly provided) the management of said property and control of the renting, handling, encumbering, selling or making any other disposition thereof, any beneficiary or his agent shall handle the rents thereof, and the proceeds of any encumbrances, sales or other disposition of said property; and the Trustee shall not be called upon to do anything in the .

management or control of said property or in respect to insurance, litigation or otherwise, except on written direction of the beneficiaries hereunder for the time being, as herein above provided, and after the payment to it of all money necessary to carry out said instructions.

5. Use of Trustee Name.

No beneficiary hereunder shall have any authority to contract for or in the name of the Trustee, or use the name of Trustee in any advertising or other publicity, or to bind the Trustee personally.

6. Term of Trust.

If the trust property or any part thereof remains in trust twenty (20) years from this date, the Trustee shall convey transfer, set over and deliver the same to the beneficiaries in accordance with their respective interests.

7. Resignation of Trustee.

The Trustee, at any time, may resign by sending by mail, a notice of its intention to do so to each of the then beneficiaries hereunder at his or her last known to the Trustee. In the event of such resignation, a Successor or Successors may be appointed by the person or persons then entitled to direct the Trustee, as to the disposition of the trust property, by an instrument in writing lodged with the resigning Trustee, having endorsed thereon the acceptance of such Successor; and thereupon the resigning Trustee shall convey the trust property to such Successor or Successors in trust.

a. In the event no Successor is appointed as herein provided, within thirty (30) days from the date of such resignation, the resigning Trustee may convey the trust property to the beneficiaries in accordance with their respective interests hereunder and thereupon this trust shall terminate. The Trustee notwithstanding such resignation shall continue to have a first lien on the trust property for its costs, expenses, including reasonable attorneys fees and for its reasonable compensation.

b. Not withstanding anything herein contained, the Trustee, at any time and without notice of any kind, may resign as to all or part of the Trustee may be subjected to embarrassment, insecurity, liability, hazard or litigation.

c. Every Successor Trustee or Trustees appointed hereunder shall become fully vested with all the estate, properties, rights, powers, trust, and duties of its, his or their predecessor.

8. Successor Trustees.

Notwithstanding anything herein contained to the contrary, in the event the Original Trustee shall die or become incapacitated, or be unwilling or unable to act for any reason, the following in order of their listing (able and willing to act) is appointed SUCCESSOR TRUSTEE with the same powers and duties of the Original Trustee.

9. Successor Trustee Recording.

Recording of this Trust Agreement and Acceptance of Successor Trustee, shall vest title in the Successor Trustee with the same powers and duties as Original Trustee. Recording shall be made in the County wherein the property held hereunder is located, and all other provisions of this trust shall remain in full force and effect.

10. Incapacitation of Successor Trustee.

Notwithstanding anything herein contained to the contrary, in the event a Successor Trustee shall die or become incapacitated, or be unwilling or unable to act for any reason, any beneficiary then living or their personal representative if deceased, may appoint a Trustee to carry out all the functions of a Trustee, with the same powers and duties of the original Trustee. Said beneficiary may name himself Successor Trustee. A copy of this Trust Agreement shall be recorded with the County Recorder wherein any property held under this trust is located, together with a statement of appointment of the new Trustee, signed by the beneficiary, or if deceased, the successor as provided herein, and if there is no named successor, said instrument may be signed by the Personal Representative of the estate of a deceased beneficiary or personal representative shall have no right, title or interest in the trust property or the beneficial interest.

11. Limitations of Liability.

All obligations incurred by the Trustee hereunder shall be secured by the trust res only and shall not be the individual obligations of either the Trustee or the beneficiary or beneficiaries.

12. Other Property Conveyed to Trustee

At any time and from time to time, additional property may be conveyed to the Trustee under this trust, and only when accepted in writing by the Trustee, shall such property and the proceeds thereof be held, dealt with and disposed of under the terms of this agreement in the manner as the property above specifically described in schedule attached hereto.

13. Compensation of Trustee.

The Trustee shall receive for its services in accepting this trust and title hereunder the sum of $_____ for the first year and the sum of $_____ for each succeeding year as long as any property remains in this trust; and it shall also receive reasonable compensation for any special services rendered by it hereunder which compensation the beneficiaries hereunder jointly and severally agree to pay.

14. Disclosure of Information.

The Trustee and the beneficiaries for the time being shall constitute the sole persons in interest under this agreement. Communications addressed by the Trustee to the beneficiaries at their last address appearing on its record shall be sufficient for all purposes. The trustee is prohibited from disclosing (a) any information concerning this trust agreement, (b) any interest in real property held in this trust and (c) identity or any information concerning the beneficiaries herein unless under court order to do so or unless such beneficiary is running for public office.

15. Disclosure to Law Enforcement Agencies.

Notwithstanding any provision of this Trust Agreement to the contrary, Florida Statute 943 dealing with Rico Liens and disclosure by the Trustee to certain law enforcement agencies shall be complied with by the Trustee in accordance with the requirements of law.

16. Acceptance.

IN TESTIMONY WHEREOF, said Trustee, accepted the duties of Trustee, the day and year last written above, and on said day the said beneficiary or beneficiaries signed this Declaration of Trust and Trust Agreement, in order to signify assent to the terms hereof.

BENEFICIARY(IES) and ADDRESS

_____

_____

Witness as to Beneficiaries

_____

_____

Witness as to Beneficiaries

_____

_____

ACCEPTED BY TRUSTEE:

_____, as Trustee and not personally.

Address:

17. Notary(ies)

STATE OF _____

COUNTY OF _____

I hereby certify that on this day, before me, an officer duly authorized in the State aforesaid and in the County aforesaid to take acknowledgments, personally appeared _____, _____, _____, _____to me known to be the person(s) described in and who executed the foregoing instrument and _____ acknowledged before me that _____ executed the same.

Witness my hand and official seal in the County and State last aforesaid this _____ day of _____ A.D., 19___ .

_____

Notary Public

My commission expires:

Chapter Sixteen

Chapter Seventeen

Two DBA Agreements

An Informal Agreement

I first started doing real estate Down Payment transactions in what I refer to as the "D.B.A." format. The investor has the properties titled in your name. This D.B.A. format can be used to buy a great number of properties all held under the same "<u>D</u>oing <u>B</u>usiness <u>A</u>s" name. This way you have a share of the profits in the entire portfolio.

There are several weaknesses to this form of agreement. First, as written, all the latitude in deciding how and when properties are going to be sold, or if they are going to be sold, leaves you without guidelines for resolving a potential disagreement concerning the disposition of the properties. One investor might be certain that you intend to sell everything for cash at the close of the agreement, while another might read the same document and assume that the active partner was going to buy out the passive partner. Still another partner might assume that you were going to divvy up the assets.

The informal nature of this agreement leads to ambiguity. Many details that you'd find in a formal agreement just aren't covered.

And finally, the wording of the contract itself might give someone the idea that you are offering a security, an interest in future profits. You don't want to become involved in security laws because qualifying for a security offering can be complex and expensive.

With all these warnings in mind, why did I bother to include this particular agreement? Because many of you will be entering into informal agreements that are no better or no worse than what I present here. If you're dealing with your mother or your children where it's virtually impossible for a dispute to erupt that couldn't be settled with very little discussion, then this format might work for you.

In fact, sometimes an informal agreement seems most appropriate. I'm offering the example only as food for thought and not as a recommended approach, and maybe you can learn from its weaknesses as much as from its content.

d/b/a AGREEMENT

_____ hereafter called "Investor", desires to make real estate investments, and is seeking a situation wherein those activities and investments will be closely monitored so as to allow the Investor freedom to continue in the Investor's current business activities and personal endeavors.

_____ hereafter called "MGR" is seeking investment partners who will allow him to manage their affairs closely and compensate him out of the profits of those investments.

It is therefore agreed that the (Investor's name) Land & Cattle Company will be formed for the purpose of holding title for the benefit of the Investor and MGR. All titles will be held in company name as a d/b/a for the Investor. The company will be formed with an initial capital of $___,000.00 paid in by the Investor.

A company checking account will be opened by MGR in the company name. MGR will select the bank or financial institution and will be the authorized signer on checks. MGR will, at his discretion, invest idle funds in interest bearing assets. MGR is hereby granted the sole power of attorney to operate the company on a day to day basis and invest the company assets.

The term of this arrangement will be five years unless mutually terminated or extended.

If so agreed, the Investor will make regular contributions to capital. However, outside of these or voluntary contributions, MGR guarantees the Investor that at no time during the term of this agreement, will the Investor be required to provide additional capital. It is intended that should additional capital be necessary, either MGR will arrange loans to continue current operations or MGR will find other investors to co-invest. At the end of the venture, MGR guarantees the Investor that the equity value of the company will equal or exceed the total investment capital paid in.

Should MGR or affiliates loan money to the company, it will earn interest at the current 90-day treasury bill rate.

MGR, in return for his efforts in this venture, will be compensated with one-half of the future profits. The profits will be distributed in cash or property at termination. MGR. will not hold title to any of the properties during the term of this agreement but will, instead, secure his claim by an option to buy a one-half, undivided interest in the company assets for $1.00, subject to the return of an amount equal to the Investors initial and subsequent investment capital(s). A notice of option in MGR's or MGR's nominee's name will be recorded with each property or asset.

MGR will not receive any of the depreciation or other tax deductions that come from ownership during the term of ownership. Any tax advantages or liabilities during the term of this agreement will be reported by the Investor as owner of the company and be a part of their taxes.

The company will not be liable to pay MGR a real estate commission for any future sales or purchases of company assets. All commissions due to MGR from the company will be paid in the form of a credit memorandum against the company. The said credit memorandum will not carry interest. Said commission will be payable if and only if the Investor has received the return of his paid capital and after the Investor has tripled his investment. Thus, if the Investor were to receive a total return of $3.00 for every $1.00 invested, the next distribution would be payment of commissions. Said payment of commission will be the only "earned income" (vs. investment gains) to be paid to MGR for MGR's time and efforts. After the commissions are paid, a further division of profits will continue on a 50/50 split basis.

Where necessary, commissions will be paid to licensed brokers or salesmen at the then going rate other than MGR. If a licensed broker, MGR may receive commissions from third parties for assets acquired by the company. However, the amount received will reduce dollar for dollar any "earned income" due MGR from the company.

Even though MGR will have the power of attorney to buy and sell, to borrow money and pay debts, to facilitate the transfer of assets, the Investor hereby agrees to sign all documents normally required if so requested.

Should MGR die prior to the termination of this agreement, _____ will act as MGR's agent to wind up the business of the company and distribute its assets. Should the Investor die prior to the termination of this agreement, the representative of the Investor and MGR shall mutually agree on the distribution of the assets.

At time of termination of the company's activities, any cash on hand or available from sale of assets shall be paid first to Investor until Investor's paid in capital is returned. Thereafter, the net asset value of the company will be distributed by mutual agreement.

All books and records of the Company will be maintained by MGR but be available to the Investor for inspection at any reasonable time. MGR will prepare all necessary support documents for the Investor's tax adviser.

The Investor will be informed of all portfolio changes from time to time as a matter of courtesy. The Investor may object to a particular portfolio move, but it is understood that this is not within the intent of this agreement and that to do so will give MGR, in his sole discretion, the right to cancel this agreement.

Should the Investor veto a portfolio move, and MGR cancel this agreement, the initial capital invested will be returned first, then any loans or advances from MGR or MGR's affiliates to the company will be paid, but under this condition, said loans to include __% annual rate interest, then MGR's commissions due plus 10% interest, thereafter all the remaining assets and money will be split 50/50. Commissions will be figured at 7% on improved property and 10% on land and mortgages.

_____   _____
The Investor   MGR

_____   _____
Dated   Dated

The Lawyers Version Of The D.B.A. Agreements

(This section gives you a very formalized, or you might say "lawyer's" version of this same agreement. It's solid to the core in legal terminology, covering every minute detail. It's also a little intimidating.)

OPTION PARTNERSHIP AGREEMENT

THIS AGREEMENT is made and entered into effective as of the ____ day of _____, 198__, by and among _____ ("Option Investor"), hereinafter collectively referred to as "Partners".

RECITALS

(i) Equity Investor desires to make investments in real estate and indebtedness secured by real estate and to have Option Investor assist him in that endeavor;

(ii) Option Investor is a licensed real estate broker in Missouri and Kansas and desires to assist Equity Investor in making real estate investments in consideration of sharing profits from such investments; and

(iii) All assets purchased by Equity Investor pursuant to this Agreement (the "Properties") shall become subject to the terms hereof and to the rights of Option Investor by virtue of this Agreement.

AGREEMENT

IN CONSIDERATION of the mutual covenants contained herein, the Partners agree as follows:

1. <u>The Partnership</u>

    1.01 <u>Name and Formation.</u>

    (a) The Partners hereby form a General Partnership (hereinafter sometimes referred to as the "Partnership") under the name of _____ Property Co.

    (b) Except as expressly provided in this Agreement to the contrary, the rights and obligations of the Partners and administration and termination of the Partnership shall be governed by the Uniform Partnership Act of the State of _____ (hereinafter the "Uniform Act". A Partner's interest in the Partnership shall be personal property for all purposes.

    1.02 <u>Term.</u> The term of the Partnership shall be five (5) years from the date of this Agreement unless terminated earlier. However, the Partners may agree to continue the Partnership beyond such term.

    1.03 <u>Purpose and Scope of the Partnership.</u>

    (a) The purpose of the Partnership shall be to acquire, own, manage and dispose of the properties.

    (b) Nothing in this Agreement shall be deemed to restrict in any way the freedom of any party to conduct any other business or activity whatsoever (including the acquisition or development of real property) even if such business or activity competes with the business of the Partnership.

    1.04 <u>Title to the Properties.</u> The title to the Properties shall be held in the name of Equity Investor d/b/a _____ Property Co., which nominee shall hold such legal title as Trustee for the sole and exclusive use and benefit of the Partnership. Option Investor shall be entitled to record a memorandum setting forth his option rights with respect to the Properties.

    .05 <u>Principal Place of Business.</u> The principal place of business of the Partnership shall be 7180 West 107th Street, Overland Park, Kansas 66212, or at such other place or places as the Partners shall designate.

1.06 <u>Scope of Partners' Authority.</u> Except as otherwise expressly and specifically provided in this Agreement, no Partner shall have any authority to act for, or assume any obligations or responsibility on behalf of, any other Partner or on behalf of the Partnership.

2. <u>Management</u>

2.01 <u>Management of the Partnership.</u>

(a) The overall management and control of the business shall be vested in the Partners. Each of the Partners shall take part in the management of the Partnership, especially as to the "Major Decisions" specified below. Option Investor shall have the responsibility and authority for conducting the ordinary and usual daily business and affairs of the Partnership as more fully set forth in Section 2.02 hereof.

(b) Notwithstanding the foregoing, no act shall be taken, sum expended, decision made or obligation incurred by the Partnership or Option Investor with respect to a matter within the scope of any of the major decisions (hereinafter called "Major Decisions"), as enumerated below, unless such Major Decision has been unanimously approved by the Partners. The Major Decisions are:

(1) Sale, transfer or encumbrance of any Properties now owned or hereafter acquired by the Partnership;

(2) The expenditure of any monies, the incurrence of any indebtedness, or the execution of any contract in excess of Five Thousand Dollars ($5,000); and

(3) All other management decisions and actions of the Partnership not specifically enumerated in Section 2.02 below.

2.02 <u>Duties of Option Investor.</u>

(a) Option Investor, at the expense of the Partnership, shall implement or cause to be implemented all Major Decisions approved by the Partners and shall conduct or cause to be conducted, through the retention of property managers or consultants, lawyers and accountants, as provided in (b) below, the operation, management, disposition or financing of the Properties in accordance with and as limited by this Agreement, including without limitation the following:

(1) Keeping all books of account and other records of the Partnership in accordance with the terms of this Agreement, including the preparation of a balance sheet and profit and loss statement semi-annually;

(2) Preparing and delivering to Equity Investor periodic reports, including tax return information (not later than March 15 of each year), not less often than annually of the state of the business and affairs of the Partnership;

(3) To the extent that funds of the Partnership are available therefore, paying all debts and other obligations of the Partnership, including amounts due under permanent and other loans of the Partnership and paying debts which are encumbrances against the Properties;

(4) Maintaining all funds of the Partnership in accounts in a bank or banks designated by the Partners;

(5) Performing other normal business functions of the Partnership in accordance with this Agreement; and

(6) Performing other obligations specified elsewhere in this Agreement to be performed by Option Investor.

(b) Option Investor shall be entitled, at the expense of the Partnership, to employ individuals to perform management, leasing, supervisory, administrative, secretarial and maintenance services for the Partnership, with the right to grant such individuals the authority to conduct ministerial acts in connection with the operation of the Properties.

(c) The Partnership shall indemnify and save harmless Option Investor from any loss, damage, liability or expense incurred or sustained by him by reason of any acts performed of its interests, it being understood, however, that the foregoing shall not relieve Option Investor from liability for gross negligence or willful malfeasance.

2.03 <u>Compensation for Management.</u> Option Investor shall not receive a salary or guaranteed fee from the Partnership. However, Option Investor may receive a real estate commission in connection with the purchase or sale of Properties with the consent of Equity Investor.

3. <u>Capital Contributions</u>

3.01 <u>Equity Investor's Contributions.</u> Equity Investor shall make the following contributions to the Partnership:

$_____ upon execution of this Agreement;

$_____ on the last day of the thirteenth month following the date of this Agreement; and

$_____ on the last day of the twenty-fifth month following the date of this Agreement.

No other capital contribution shall be required of Equity Investor. However, Option Investor may require Equity Investor to execute mortgages, deeds of trust and other security instruments affecting the Properties in connection with loans to the Partnership.

3.02 Option Investor's Contributions. During the term of the Partnership, Option Investor shall not be required to make any capital contribution to the Partnership. However, Option Investor shall loan money to the Partnership or execute all notes for borrowings by the Partnership needed to obtain funds in excess of Equity Investor's contributions.

3.03 Option Investor's Option. Option Investor has the right to acquire a one half interest in all profits realized by the Partnership as determined by the amount of all Partnership funds plus the net fair market value of all Properties in excess of the book capital account of Equity Investor. Option Investor shall exercise such right by contributing $1.00 to the Partnership.

3.04 No Interest on Capital. No interest shall be payable on the capital contribution of any Partner nor shall any Partner have the right to withdraw his capital contributions.

4. Partners' Capital Accounts

4.01 Book Capital Accounts. A separate book capital account shall be maintained for each Partner. Each such account shall be credited with an amount equal to the net fair market value of any assets and the amount of cash contributed by each Partner. Each such account shall be debited only in the amount of any cash distribution or distribution of property to a Partner in an amount agreed upon as the net fair market value of such property distributed.

4.02 Tax Basis Capital Accounts. A separate tax basis capital account shall be maintained for each Partner. Such tax basis capital account shall be credited with an amount equal to the basis for tax purposes of all assets contributed by a Partner and by the amount of cash contributed by a Partner. Such account shall be credited and debited in accordance with the allocation of profits and losses as set forth in Section 5 below.

5. Partnership Interests

5.01 Allocation of Profits and Losses.

(a) All losses of the Partnership shall be allocated in direct proportion to the book capital accounts of the Partners.

(b) Until Equity Investor's tax basis capital account equals his book capital account, all profits shall be allocated to Equity Investor. Thereafter, all profits shall be allocated equally between the Partners, unless Option Investor elects not to exercise his option pursuant to Section 3.03, in which case all profits shall be allocated to Equity Investor.

5.02 <u>Distributions to Partners.</u> If requested and approved by the Partners, Option Investor shall distribute the Cash forth in this Section 5.02. For the purposes of this Agreement "Cash Available for Distribution" shall be the taxable income of the Partnership for Federal income tax purposes plus depreciation and other non-cash charges deducted in determining such taxable income minus (i) principal payments on all mortgages and other secured and unsecured indebtedness, (ii) repair and maintenance reserves and capital expenditures when made from other than such reserves, (iii) any other cash expenditures (except distributions to Partners) which have not been deducted in determining the taxable income of the Partnership, and (iv) any amount required to maintain reasonable working capital as determined by Option Investor. Distributions made from Cash Available for Distribution shall be made in the following order:

(a) All cash Available for Distribution shall be paid to Equity Investor until such time as his book capital account equals zero.

(b) The next Cash Available for Distribution shall be paid to Option Investor until such time as his book capital account equals zero.

(c) All distributions thereafter shall be made equally to the Partners.

5.03 <u>Access to Books.</u> Each Partner shall have the right at all reasonable times during usual business hours to audit, examine and make copies of or extracts from the books of account of the Partnership. Such rights may be exercised through any agent or employee of such Partner designated by such Partner. Each Partner shall bear all expenses incurred in any examination made for such Partner's account.

6. <u>Termination</u>

6.01 <u>Voluntary Dissolution and Automatic Dissolution.</u>

(a) Anything, in this Agreement to the contrary notwithstanding, the powers of the parties hereto to effect a dissolution of the Partnership at any time shall be governed by the provisions of the Uniform Act, but this shall not be construed to authorize nor shall any Partner have the right to withdraw or retire from the Partnership or to cause a dissolution of the Partnership or to cause a dissolution of the Partnership except as elsewhere in this Agreement expressly provided.

(b) If Equity Investor shall disapprove any Major Decision proposed by Option Investor, then Option Investor may terminate this Agreement upon thirty (30) days' written notice.

(c) The death, adjudicated incompetency or bankruptcy of any Partner shall immediately dissolve the Partnership, but the Partnership shall be deemed automatically reconstituted and the business of the Partnership shall be carried on without interruption and without the execution of any confirmatory agreement as a new Partnership under the same name and under the same terms and provisions as are set forth in this Agreement until the personal representative or successor of such Partner shall elect to terminate the Partnership.

6.02 <u>Rights of Option Investor Upon Termination</u>

(a) If the Partnership is terminated prior to the end of its term pursuant to paragraph (b) of Section 6.01, then Option Investor may elect to sell his option rights to Equity Investor at a price equal to 50% of the actual and potential profit realized or to be realized by the Partnership. Such profit shall be determined by computing the total value of all assets, including the Properties (notes shall be valued at par and real estate shall be valued at fair market value by independent appraisal), less all Partnership liabilities and the book capital account of Equity Investor. If the purchase price is not paid in cash within sixty (60) days of the termination, Option Investor may elect to receive Properties at their net fair market value in lieu of all or part of the purchase price.

(b) If the Partnership shall be otherwise dissolved and terminated as provided in this Agreement, the affairs of the Partnership shall be wound up, and, during the winding up period and until such time as the Partnership's interest in the Properties have been sold and the proceeds therefrom collected and distributed, the authority of Option Investor shall continue and the rights and obligations of the Partners and other persons owning an interest in the Partnership shall be governed and controlled by all the provisions of this Agreement.

6.03 <u>Distribution on Liquidation.</u> In the event of the sale or other disposition in one transaction of all or substantially all the assets of the Partnership, of the condemnation of the Properties, or of the termination of the Partnership, the Partnership shall be dissolved and liquidated and all the assets of the Partnership shall be distributed in the following order of priority:

(a) all the Properties, if any, shall be sold or collected and turned into cash as expeditiously as possible;

(b) all the Partnership's debts, liabilities and obligations (excluding any loans or advances by the Partners) shall be paid in full or reserves therefore shall be set aside;

(c) all the Partnership's debts, liabilities and obligations to the Partners shall be paid, but if the amount available therefore shall be insufficient, then prorata on account thereof;

(d) the cash remaining after the payment of the items referred to in paragraph

(c) above shall be distributed to the Partners and any other persons owning an interest in the Partnership in accordance with Section 5.01.

7. General

7.01 Notices

(a) All notices, demands, requests or consents provided for or permitted to be given pursuant to this Agreement must be in writing. All notices, demands and requests to be sent to any Partner pursuant hereto shall be deemed to have been properly given or served by depositing the same in the United States mail addressed to such Partner, postpaid and certified with return receipt requested, at the address designated below the signature of such Partner.

(b) All notices, demands and requests shall be effective upon being deposited in the United States mail. However, the time period in which a response to any such notice, demand or request must be given shall commence to run from the date of receipt on the return receipt of the notice, demand or request by the addressee thereof. Rejection or other refusal to accept or the inability to deliver because of changed address of which not notice was given shall be deemed to be receipt of the notice, demand or request sent.

7.02 Governing Law

This Agreement and the obligations of the Partners and their successors and assigns hereunder shall be interpreted, construed and enforced in accordance with the laws of the State of _____.

7.03 Entire Agreement.

This Agreement contains the entire agreement among the parties hereto relative to the formation of the Partnership. No variations, modifications or changes herein or hereof shall be binding upon any party unless set forth in a document duly executed by or on behalf of such property.

7.04 Waiver.

No consent or waiver, express or implied, by any Partner to any breach or default by any other Partner in the performance by such other Partner of his obligations under this Agreement shall be deemed or construed to be a consent or waiver to or of any other breach or default in the performance by such other Partner of the same or any other obligations of such Partner hereunder. Failure on the part of any Partner to complain of any act or failure to act of the other Partner or to declare the other Partner in default, irrespective of how long such failure continues, shall not constitute a waiver by such Partner of his rights under this Agreement.

7.05 Binding Agreement.

This Agreement shall inure to the benefit of and be binding upon the undersigned Partners and their respective heirs, executors, legal representatives, successors and assigns.

IN WITNESS WHEREOF, each of the Partners has executed this Agreement as of the day and year first above written.

NAME AND ADDRESS   SIGNATURE

_____

_____

_____   _____

_____

_____

_____   _____

_____

_____

_____   _____

_____

_____   _____

Chapter Eighteen

Syndicating Options

Joint Venture Options

If the potential profits warrant a major cash outlay to acquire an option, and you don't have the money to do it by yourself, why not syndicate the option?

An investment group can purchase an asset, any asset, including an option. The option, or the right to acquire the subject real estate, will become the asset of the partnership.

The potential benefits can be spread in proportion to contributions with or without special consideration to the person who put the transaction together. In many transactions the individual who formulated and organized the investment group gets a "free ride." A "free ride" refers to a share of the future profits without having to make an investment.

You can put together whatever compensation format you want. In the document at hand, I have traded equity in a resort condominium for the initial consideration necessary to obtain the option. Additional cash payments were necessary, so I syndicated the option to raise the necessary cash.

The agreement follows on next page.

PARTNERSHIP AGREEMENT

This Partnership Agreement is made and entered into as of _____ , 19___ by and among_____,
(hereinafter referred to as "_____") and
_____,
_____
_____,
_____
_____,
_____
_____,
_____
_____ hereinafter referred to as "Investors").

1. *Name*
The name of the partnership shall be
_____ .

2. *Place of Business*
The principal place of business shall be at _____ and at such other place or places as may be agreed upon by the partners.

3. *Purpose*
The purpose of the partnership is to purchase and acquire quire from _____ all of its right, title and interest in and to an Option to Purchase from _____ certain land located in_____ all of which is more fully described in the Option to Purchase dated _____ .

4. *Term*
The partnership shall commence on _____ and shall continue until terminated as hereinafter provided. The partnership shall operate on a calendar year for accounting purposes.

5. *Capital*

5.01 *Initial Contributions.* The initial capital of the partnership shall consist of a total of
_____ ($ .00 DOLLARS)
contributed by the partners in the following amounts:

Name of Investor Amount of Initial Contribution

_____ $ _____
_____ $ _____
_____ $ _____

_____	$ _____
_____	$ _____
_____	$ _____
_____	$ _____
_____	$ _____
_____	$ _____
_____	$ _____

5.02 *Additional Contributions.* Each Investor shall contribute his pro rata share of _____ ($ 000.00) DOLLARS on or before _____ 19___ . In each of the calendar years 19_____ and 19_____ each Investor shall pay his pro rata share of_____ ($ 000.00) DOLLARS provided that written notice is sent by_____ each Investor requesting such payment on or before_____ of that year, and payments shall be made on or before _____ of such year in which notice is received requesting the additional contribution.

5.03 *Default.* In the event an Investor does not make any of the additional contributions provided in Section 5.02 within the time period provided, the remaining Investors shall be notified by _____ and, during the fifteen (15) day period following the date of such notice, shall be entitled to make his pro rata share of the contribution which was to be made by the defaulting Investor. In the event the full amount of the contribution is not subscribed by the remaining Investors, then _____ may pay all or any part of the contribution of the defaulting Investor. Upon default, an Investor shall no longer be considered a partner, but shall become a creditor of the partnership. His capital account shall be assigned to those Investors and/or ____ in the same proportion in which they have made contributions on his behalf. Upon termination of the partnership, if any distribution is made with respect to the capital accounts of any partner, then the defaulting Investor shall receive the full amount which he has invested in the partnership prior to the date of his default, but shall not be entitled to receive any profits over and above the amount of his investment.

6. *Profits and Losses*

In the event of a loss by the partnership, the Investors shall be entitled to share in such loss in the same proportion as their contributions to the partnership. In the event of any profit earned by the partnership from any source other than the sale or other disposition of the Option to Purchase, the Investors shall share in such profit in the same proportion as their contributions to the partnership. In the event of any profit realized from the sale or disposition of the Option to Purchase or in the event of the exercise of the Option to Purchase and upon any sale or disposition of the Contract for Deed, or the property subject to the Contract for Deed, the Investors shall first receive the amounts of their capital accounts, and any profit over and above the capital accounts shall be distributed fifty (50%) percent to _____ and fifty (50%) percent to the Investors in proportion to their capital accounts.

7. *Management*

7.01 *Assessment for Expenses*. It is anticipated that the initial capital contribution of $ .00 will be sufficient to make the initial purchase of the Option to Purchase and pay out-of-pocket expenses incurred in connection with the formation of the partnership and for any other expenses, including preparation of tax returns throughout the life of the partnership. There shall be no assessment for expenses of the partnership without the unanimous consent of all Investors. Any expenses of the partnership in excess of the amount of the contributions of the Investors set forth above shall be paid by_____.

7.02 *No Compensation*. No compensation shall be paid to any Investor or ____ except for reimbursement of reasonable out-of-pocket expenses incurred on behalf of the partnership to the extent limited in the foregoing sub-section and as provided in Section 6.

7.03 *Duties of* ____ . ____ shall be responsible for and have the authority to exercise all rights and privileges of the optionee under the Option to Purchase and to take all necessary action and steps for complying with any of the requirements of the optionee pursuant to the Option to Purchase. ____ shall also keep the partnership books and be responsible for the preparation and filing of the necessary tax returns for the partnership.

7.04 *Bank Account*. A bank account for the partnership shall be opened and withdrawals may be made in the name of the partnership by the signature of any duly authorized officer of _____.

8. *Disposition of Partnership Assets*

8.01 *Authority of* ____ . ____ shall have the full authority to act on behalf of the partnership in connection with any sale or other disposition of the Option to Purchase, the Contract for Deed, or the underlying property at such price and upon such terms as it shall deem advisable.

8.02 *No Individual Disposition of Partnership Assets* The Investors shall have no right to specific assets of the partnership, but shall have only the right as partners to an undivided interest in assets of the partnership. No Investor shall enter into any agreement or negotiate for any sale or disposition of any assets of the partnership or incur any liability on behalf of the partnership without the specific written authorization of _____ .

9. *Withdrawal or Dissolution*

9.01 *Voluntary Withdrawal*. In the event any Investor desires to withdraw from the partnership prior to its termination he shall give written notice to ____ at least ninety (90) days in advance of the effective date of the withdrawal. ____ shall give written notice of such desire to the other Investors within thirty (30) days thereafter and the remaining Investors shall have the right to purchase the capital account of the withdrawing Partner on a pro rata basis. In the event the remaining Investors do not agree to acquire the entire capital account of the withdrawing partner within thirty(30) days of the date of the notice from _____ , then_____ may acquire any or all of such withdrawing Investor's interest by notifying the withdrawing Investor within sixty (60) days after the date of the initial notice of the desire to withdraw. The purchase price of the capital account of the withdrawing Investor shall be equal to and payable upon the same terms as any bona fide offer received by the withdrawing Investor from any third party for the purchase of such capital account. If the right of first refusal set forth herein is not exercised by the remaining Investors or___, then the withdrawing Investor may complete the sale of his capital account to the third person upon the terms and conditions set forth in the original notice to____, but the person acquiring such capital account shall subscribe to and be bound by the terms of this Agreement. In the event the withdrawing Investor has not received a bona fide offer to purchase his capital account by any third person, then the purchase price shall be the amount of his capital account on the date the withdrawal becomes effective which amount may be paid at the termination of the partnership.

9.02 Death. In the event of the death of any one of the Investors, the partnership shall continue and the estate or heirs of the deceased Investor shall be entitled to all of the rights and privileges of the deceased Investor and shall be responsible for all of the obligations of the deceased Investor.

9.03 Dissolution. This partnership may be dissolved by agreement of all the parties, upon written notice by_____ to all Investors or upon the dissolution, liquidation or insolvency of _____. In the event of dissolution, after payment of all partnership liabilities to third parties, the remaining assets of the partnership shall be distributed as follows:

a. All liabilities to defaulting Investors shall be paid;

b. Individual capital accounts of non-defaulting Investors shall be paid; and

c. The balance shall be divided among the Investors and _____ in accordance with the provisions in Sec. 6 above.

_____ DATE:
_____ DATE:
_____ DATE:
_____ DATE:
_____ DATE:
_____ DATE:
_____ DATE:
_____ DATE:
_____ DATE:

There are some state and federal regulations that apply to syndications--be sure to obtain complete legal review.

Usually there are exceptions for only two types of people in a deal--but don't assume anything when it comes to securities.

There are some exceptions for small deals involving knowledgeable or wealthy investors.

Standard forms should not be used without legal review.

Here's another version of a joint venture for an option.

EXAMPLE: You find a tremendous bargain, a piece of property worth $200,000 and you get an option to buy it for $120,000. What's the value of the option? $80,000. If the option is going to cost you $20,000 there is still some profit there.

YOUR OFFER TO OTHER INVESTORS: "How would you like a half interest in an option? You put up $20,000 for this $80,000 option and you'll have a half interest in it. Your half interest is worth $40,000."

To make them feel more secure, you might add, "in fact, when we sell we'll give you the first $20,000 out so that you are somewhat protected."

Thus, if the property only netted $25,000, $20,000 would be returned to the cash investors first. **Without that clause, they would only get $12,500.**

Chapter Nineteen

Shared Appreciation Mortgages

You Can Do It With An Option

As the lease with option to buy became more popular, a new system evolved called SAM (Shared Appreciation Mortgage). Now the shared appreciation mortgage was a concept the pension funds really went for initially, but it hasn't caught on like I thought it would or like it probably should have.

Here's the concept of a shared appreciation mortgage. If you went to buy a piece of property and you are looking at paying over 10% interest on the fixed rate loan, you probably wouldn't qualify if you're the average American.

(The ownership of a home is a very, very personal thing. The ownership of where you live has bottom line benefits that can't be equated financially. It is the quality of life - who your neighbors are, what school your children go to, what country club you can or cannot belong to because of the area you live in. All these things.)

Yes, it is better to have 100% appreciation of the house you live in. But if you can't afford it alone, it is next best to be able to live in the house and have some of the appreciation.

Here's what the mortgage company would say. "Normally we'd ask 11%." (I'm just using these round numbers to make the example easy on our 30 year mortgage.) "You say you can't afford it. Fine. We'll only charge you 10% and we'll take one-third of the future appreciation. *That means as the property goes up in value, two-thirds of the appreciation is yours and one-third is mine.* When we sell, first we'll give you the down payment back and the pay down on the loan. Then we'll take one-third of the net proceeds that are left above that as additional interest .

This worked great for the pension funds because they wanted a fixed dollar return. They wanted to know that the money was coming in regularly so they could fund all their obligations plus they wanted to have a little bonus, a little flake of an inflation hedge. And, this was it. Coastal State's Savings and Loan in Florida came out with an issue of, I believe, five million dollars worth of first mortgages like this and they were gone in something like 12 hours of business because customers wanted them that much. Now why haven't they caught fire?

During the early 1980's prices were somewhat flat for real estate. You didn't see the normal appreciation. That was the apple that was attracting the pension funds.

Advanced Mortgage Corporation said if you gave them 20 million dollars they would buy the mortgages for you. They would put it together and guarantee service on these mortgages. Otherwise, if there were any delinquencies or deficiencies they would handle it. They would send you a check on a monthly basis and you'd get one-third of the appreciation plus the guaranteed return.

The pension funds loved it but when the proceeds from this mortgage were 10% and seeing no appreciation in markets in 1981 and 1982, they decided to go back and pick up the 17%-18% straight 30-year mortgage. They just couldn't resist the lure of the high fixed return. They're saying when they see inflation start to heat up again they will go back into this market and do it again. But it is a tremendous idea.

I first saw this idea in action about the time I was trying to do the same thing by myself. I was trying to do an owner carry back shared appreciation mortgage and I must admit I fumbled around with it.

So, to structure my own SAM I went to a seller. The seller had a group of 10 houses he wanted to sell. He said he would take a little bit of money down and 12% fully amortized financing.

As is often the case, the reason he was selling was because he couldn't fire his property manager (his son), and his concern was he didn't have much income coming in. He had renewed leases year after year with no increases because the son was lazy.

I knew when I hopped into this I was going to have a horrendous negative cash flow.

I looked at him and thought, Boy! These are not going to just be alligators, these are going to be papa gators! I told him I would buy these units from him and pay him 6% interest plus half the appreciation. It sounded like a great idea but how do you structure that?

We sat down to work, because this guy liked to work out problems too, and part of my closing technique was to get him involved in this. The solution we came up with wasn't a real happy one.

What it really amounted to was - if I gave him 6% interest plus half the future appreciation, the IRS would probably say that it was ordinary income instead of capital gains. That is something he didn't really want.

Chapter Nineteen

If you do a shared appreciation loan I think you are going to find the well has been salted by Advanced Mortgage Corporation and others because their documents include "plus a share of the future interest."

My second attempt was very successful. Unlike the first seller, this one was highly motivated. He wasn't worried about the fact that the return on his money would be taxed at ordinary income rates. Here's the story.

EXAMPLE: The seller, Mr. Stone, first approached me as a potential buyer because the properties were fairly close to Kansas City. He lived hundreds of miles away. At first I wasn't much interested.

A month later he came back to town and urged me to make an offer. I half jokingly said, "How about ten years, no payments." He countered, "Well, how would you figure the interest?"

I then realized he was serious. "We could either accumulate the interest at a fixed rate or, calculate it to be 25% of profits. A shared appreciation mortgage." We discussed the idea further and he seemed to like it.

Here is the essence of what we agreed to after six months of negotiations.

SOLUTION: I bought the properties. There were 36 units — both duplexes and single family houses. Five years was to be the length of the shared appreciation period. Those of you who have heard or read my series know how much I hate balloon payments. So, we also agreed that if the notes (one note per house) were not paid in five years, there would be an appraisal to establish the debt to the seller. (If the property value in those five years goes from a purchase price of $50,000 to an appreciated value of $100,000, the seller would be due the original amount of the note plus $25,000.) The new amount due, as determined by the appraisal, would be treated as a fully amortized note. Mr. Stone agreed to 20 years at 10% interest!

The deal we stuck sounds almost too good to be true. In part, it was. At the time of sale, Mr. Stone was $60,000 behind in payments, taxes etc, thus, the soft terms. This deal is as soft as any I ever expect to get. The terms you can get will vary with each deal.

If I were a seller, and most mortgages were at 14%, I would ask for 10% interest paid monthly plus a percentage of the profits. As a buyer, I only offer a percentage and never mention guaranteed interest payments.

Your documents that will allow you to complete a shared appreciation transaction can be a contract for deed or land sales as well as a Deed of Trust or a Mortgage.

Chapter Nineteen

You can just mention the share of future profits due you in the note and define how the number is derived. Or, you can receive any standard mortgage instrument and AN OPTION.

The option would be drawn to give the holder the right to buy a predetermined percentage of the property for $1 above the existing mortgages.

If the property was currently worth $500,000, (let's say it was a small office), you could give a $200,000 second at a low interest rate and also receive an option to purchase 25% in the property for $1 plus one-fourth the first and second mortgage balances AT TIME OF EXERCISE OF THE OPTION. This structure, as with the "Down Payment Partner" concept, will allow you 25% of the future profits.

I have made offers ranging from 25-50% of the appreciation. The amount I am willing to offer depends on whether the the price is at a premium or at a bargain, and the quality of the investment.

The advantages are obvious. For a buyer, paying for the use of the money with appreciation only is a lifesaver when you are worried about the negative cash flow. Even coupled with an interest requirement, cash flow is improved.

For a seller, it could be a super inflation hedge. Also, if a seller can get a higher price with a S.A.M., then more of his or her return would be capital gains. And, the shared appreciation is not taxed until received. This could be of special help if the seller was in a high tax now and expects that bracket to be lower later.

And this is a true win-win formula. If you are buying a property and need low interest rate financing, you could attract such a deal by "sweetening the pot" by giving the lender a share the profit option.

This option format for a Shared Appreciation Mortgage has one advantage over the approach where you recite the share of profit in the mortgage. If the option format is used, you can sell or trade the note and keep the option! If you are any good at getting full value out of notes when you sell or trade them, you could keep all the gravy at a very low price!

Chapter Nineteen

POSTSCRIPT

The option is one of the most flexible tools in real estate.

We've defined it, discussed its structure, and cited countless ways to make an option work for you, with lots of clout and little out-of-pocket money. And, there are precise documents herein to help you write up your own options, with optional clauses to include for added protection.

As with so may other real estate financing and/or acquisition techniques, **you need the knowledge BEFORE YOU ARE ABLE TO SEE THE OPPORTUNITIES.** And don't be hesitant about hiring competent legal assistance.

Now, the door to option opportunities should be open to you!

Bernard Zick, CCIM